I CALL
BULLSHIT

I CALL

DEBUNKING
THE MOST COMMONLY
REPEATED MYTHS

JAMIE FRATER

Ulysses Press

Published in the United States by
ULYSSES PRESS
P.O. Box 3440
Berkeley, CA 94703
www.ulyssespress.com

ISBN 978-1-56975-985-1
Library of Congress Control Number 2011926025

Acquisitions Editor: Keith Riegert
Managing Editor: Claire Chun
Project Manager: Alice Riegert
Copyeditor: Barbara Schultz
Proofreader: Abigail Reser
Production: Judith Metzener
Front cover design: Double R Design
Back cover design: what!design @ whatweb.com
Cover photos: smiling man © ULTRA_GENERIC/istockphoto.com,
    dunce © amdandy/istockphoto.com
Interior photos: see page 252

Printed in the United States by Bang Printing

10 9 8 7 6 5 4 3 2 1

Distributed by Publishers Group West

To anyone who has had to unlearn the misconceptions by which they have been deceived.

CONTENTS

ACKNOWLEDGMENTS

Three years after the launch of Listverse, we are now seeing our third book in print. For that monumental achievement I have to thank all of the contributors to Listverse, be they editors, writers, or administrators. Also a debt of thanks is owed to the supportive readers who have made it all possible.

I would also like to thank all of the staff at Ulysses Press for their efforts and assistance in the preparation and publication of our books. They have all been supportive, professional, and, most importantly, friendly.

And finally I must thank all of my family members, loved ones, and friends for their seemingly infinite patience when listening to me rant about the latest bit of trivia I have scraped up in my constant search for new material.

MYTH MSG (monosodium glutamate) is bad for your health and makes you sick.

BULLSHIT! MSG has a bad reputation for being harmful to health, but it is actually quite safe. MSG is a naturally occurring substance found in produce such as tomatoes, mushrooms, and seaweed. It was first isolated and presented in pure powder form in 1907 and 1909, respectively. MSG is a flavor enhancer that excites the fifth taste sense, umami (the others being salty, sweet, sour, and bitter). MSG is to umami as sugar is to sweet. Another term for umami (and a relatively good description of it) is "savory." When you add MSG to a bland soup or stock, it can greatly increase the flavor and add a roundness that can not be obtained elsewhere. Most fine chefs will use natural MSG when possible—through the inclusion of tomatoes or mushrooms—but many will also use the powder.

Thanks to media scares around the world, people have a great horror of MSG, but those same people have no problems scarfing chips and other fast food and prepackaged foods, almost all of which contain MSG. A quick survey of supermarket shelves will reveal that most packaged seasonings and sauces contain MSG. An Australian study on "Chinese Restaurant Syndrome" shows no connection: "rigorous and realistic scientific evidence linking the syndrome to MSG could not be found." Enjoy MSG!

MYTH   There are traces of urine on bar nuts.

BULLSHIT!   Apparently a scientific study on peanuts in bars found traces of more than 100 unique specimens of urine. But after a rigorous search for more information, it turns out that no scientific study (or non-scientific study for that matter) has ever been conducted on peanuts at bars. However, in the United Kingdom, there was a study done on ice cubes in bars in 2003. The study discovered that 44 percent of ice cubes tested contained coliform bacteria—bacteria that comes from human poop. Even more shockingly, 5 percent were infected with the potentially deadly E. coli bacteria. I guess that proves that they aren't making their ice cubes from bottled water. So, next time you are in London, pass on the ice and enjoy some peanuts instead.

MYTH Specific tastes correspond to specific parts of the tongue.

BULLSHIT! Contrary to popular belief, different tastes can be detected on all parts of the tongue. The original "tongue map" was based on a Harvard psychologist's mistranslation of a German paper that was written in 1901. Sensitivity to all tastes occurs across the whole tongue as well as in other regions of the mouth where there are taste, like the epiglottis and soft palate.

MYTH Haggis, the national dish of Scotland, is Scottish.

BULLSHIT! It turns out that haggis (that tasty dish of minced lamb's heart, lungs, and liver) is an import to Scotland, most likely from Scandinavia, and it arrived long before Scotland was even a nation. In fact, even the Romans used to eat a very similar dish, and it is mentioned in Homer's *Odyssey*: "A man before a great blazing fire turning swiftly this way and that a stomach full of fat and blood, very eager to have it roasted quickly." While we are on the subject, bagpipes are not Scottish either: They were described in ancient writings of the Hittites (from present day Turkey), and kilts—though not tartans—were introduced to Scotland by the Vikings.

MYTH   Spinach makes you strong—like Popeye the Sailor Man!

BULLSHIT!   Actually…it doesn't. This myth comes from the belief that spinach is high in iron,

which is false. Believe it or not, this part of the myth comes from a handwriting error in 1870, when a Doctor Wolf accidentally put a decimal point in the wrong place and made it look like spinach had ten times more iron that it really does. Now to the strong part of the myth: In order to get muscle strength, you need to exercise and do weight training. Eating spinach (or anything else, for that matter) won't make you strong on its own; it will only give you the energy you need to survive your workout.

MYTH Six meals a day is healthier than three.

BULLSHIT! A relatively recent diet phenomenon involves switching from three to six meals per day. This can be okay—but only if you are extremely good at controlling your portion sizes; it is all too easy to turn six small meals into six large meals. This myth again comes down to the whole "calories per day" rule. If your three large meals contain as many calories as your six small meals, there is no difference at all. For the majority of people, it is easier to put the time aside for three meals, so this is still the best choice for most. The time of day that you eat does not have a bearing on weight gain or loss.

MYTH High-fructose corn syrup (HFCS) is making us fat.

BULLSHIT!   HFCS entered the American food supply in the 1970s, and the rates of obesity started to rise about then. Consequently, many blame HFCS for the fat plague. It's true, of course, that the calories HFCS contributes can be linked to the nation's obesity problems, but in terms of calorie count, it's no

different from refined white sugar: The makeup of HFCS (55 percent fructose and 45 percent glucose) is close to that of white sugar (50 percent fructose and 50 percent glucose), which means that our bodies digest HFCS and sugar in very similar ways. Nutritionally speaking, the two are virtually identical. Interesting fact: Coca-Cola produced in Mexico is still made with sugar (as opposed to corn syrup in the U.S.), and many people claim to be able to taste the difference—refusing to buy the "inferior" American coke. Unfortunately, a truly scientific blind test has not been done and the various tests to be found online vary widely in their conclusions.

MYTH   Coffee helps sober a person up.

BULLSHIT!   Alcohol is metabolized by the body at a constant rate (one unit of around one-third ounce per hour), and you can't do anything to make it happen faster. Beer contains two units of alcohol per pint, so if you drink two pints, it will take four hours for your blood alcohol level to return to zero. All coffee will do is make you a wide-awake drunk, just as a cold shower will make you a wet drunk. All you can do is settle down and wait for the effects to pass naturally.

MYTH   Margarine is one molecule away from plastic.

BULLSHIT!   This is a ridiculous statement. Americans eat four times as much margarine as butter every year, which seems surprising considering so many people believe this little myth about the oil-based spread. While a lot of the negative stuff we hear about margarine is true, this particular myth is not. Margarine is made by heating vegetable oil and infusing it with hydrogen—in other words, saturating it to a point where it remains hard at room temperature, meaning the margarine is simply a white lump that resembles fat. Yellow food coloring is added and voilà—we have margarine. There is not one molecule of anything that you could add to margarine to turn it into plastic. Interesting fact: Margarine was invented in 1869 when Emperor Louis Napoleon III of France offered a prize to anyone who could come up with a cheap butter alternative for the army and the lower classes. Hippolyte Mège-Mouriés, a French chemist, won the prize with his oleomargarine. Governments around the world tried to stop people from using margarine by putting heavy taxes on it and banning its coloring. Believe it or not, it is still illegal to sell butter-colored margarine in Missouri, and it was illegal in Quebec until July 2008.

MYTH   Absinthe is poisonous.

BULLSHIT!   Absinthe was never any more poisonous than whiskey. This myth goes back at least to the 1800s and claims that it causes hallucinations—as potently as LSD—and fries the brain.

Not true. Absinthe is manufactured from *Artemisia absinthium*, a plant that has no poisons in it. It is very bitter, like the Greek liquor ouzo, and the distillation process routinely results in absinthe proofs of 100 to 180 (50 to 90 percent alcohol by volume). This

MYTH   Danish pastries are Danish.

BULLSHIT!   Arguably the world's most misleadingly named food, Danish pastries actually originated in Austria and were inspired by Turkish baklava. Their name comes from Danish chef L. C. Klitteng, who popularized them in western Europe and the United States in the early 20th century. He even baked "Danish" for the wedding of President Woodrow Wilson in 1915. In Denmark and much of Scandinavia, Danish pastries are called "Viennese bread." During the Islamic cartoon controversy of 2006, Danish pastries were renamed "Roses of the Prophet Muhammad" in Iran due to their association with the offending country.

is significantly stronger than the average whiskey, but will not produce any effect in the drinker other than drunkenness. The truth, though, is that during the Moulin Rouge days of Toulouse-Lautrec and van Gogh, starving artists liked getting drunk and couldn't afford the good stuff. So they bought absinthe from cheap street vendors, who did not care if they sold contaminated products. Cyanide and strychnine were found in this absinthe and did cause hallucinations. Today, absinthe is legal in the U. S., and perfectly safe to drink if bought commercially.

MYTH Caffeine stunts your growth.

BULLSHIT! Caffeine will do a lot of negative things to you, but it will not stunt your growth. It has nothing to do with growth. Experiments have shown that children who consume caffeine do not grow any more slowly than children who are not allowed caffeine over a period of years. The myth was probably dreamed up by some clever parent who didn't want his child drinking so much Pepsi.

MYTH   Fat-free food is calorie-free.

BULLSHIT!   This is a very common myth—so common that food manufacturers market to it. The misconception that fat-free is better is the reason that so many products are labeled "fat-free," "low in fat," "reduced fat," etc. So many people who want to lose weight will chow down on all of these "low-fat" foods thinking they are going to lose weight, but the result is even worse: They often tend to eat more of the low-fat food than they would have if it were full fat. What really matters when trying to reduce weight is calories—eat fewer calories than you burn and you will lose weight. When fat is removed from food, a lot of the flavor is removed as well. Consequently, extra sugars and chemicals are often added to increase the flavor. Fat-free food can therefore be far worse and more fattening for you than regular full-fat food.

MYTH   Drinking alcohol warms you up.

BULLSHIT!   It is commonly seen in movies as an antidote to coldness, and people still believe the myth about the Saint Bernard dogs with casks of liquor around their necks. However, when you drink alcohol, your body temperature actually drops! This is because alcohol allows more blood to reach the surface of the body, and more heat is radiated or conducted away. Any feeling of warmth experienced after drinking alcohol is explained by the fact that this flow of blood to the surface warms the skin and the ends of the sensory nerves in the skin, and these convey to the brain a sensation of warmth. The fact that alcohol actually lowers the temperature of the body was first announced by Sir B. Ward Richardson in 1866 to the British Association.

MYTH *Sushi* means raw fish.

BULLSHIT! *Sushi* does not mean raw fish, and not all sushi includes raw fish. The Japanese term for raw fish is *sashimi*. The word *sushi* actually

refers to the way the rice is prepared with a vinegary dressing. Toppings for the rice may traditionally include not only raw fish, but also cooked seafood, fish roe, egg, or vegetables such as cucumber, daikon radish, or ume plum. The dish constituting sushi and other fillings wrapped in seaweed is referred to as *makizushi*, not sushi.

MYTH   Fast-food salads are a "healthy option."

BULLSHIT!   A 2005 report by the British newspaper the *Independent* said, "[A]n investigation of the food sold by the 'big four'—McDonald's, Burger King, KFC, and Pizza Hut—found that [...] five out of eight of the salads used as 'evidence' of their embrace of healthy eating had 'high' salt or fat content." It is all too common to see dieters who crave a little something naughty ordering salads or other "healthy choices" from fast-food joints. What they usually don't realize is that the salads can be as bad as the regular food, and they would be more content if they just ate a Big Mac. For the sake of comparison, I looked it up: At McDonald's one Big Mac has 540 calories and 1,040 mg of salt; one premium Southwest salad with crispy chicken and dressing has 530 calories and 1,260 mg of salt. The Big Mac is healthier.

MYTH Fresh fruit is better for your health than dried fruit.

BULLSHIT! This myth is true in only one regard: If you are looking for vitamin C, then fresh fruit is best, but other than that, dried fruit contains just as many nutrients and sugar for energy as fresh fruit. If you subscribe to the notion that you should eat five fruits a day, then you only need one tablespoon of dried fruit per portion—so five tablespoons of dried fruit fulfills your daily need. The same is true of canned or frozen fruit. Fruit juice can also be considered a daily fruit portion, but only one serving per day should be made up of juice only.

MYTH When trying to gain muscle, you should eat copious amounts of protein.

BULLSHIT! This myth is so widespread that it doesn't look like it will die anytime soon. But according to the Mayo Clinic, 10 to 35 percent of your daily dietary intake should be protein—whether you're trying to gain weight, lose weight, or maintain your current weight. Most of this protein comes from our regular food, and we seldom need to take protein supplements. Even more damning for this myth are two recent studies by independent sports medicine journals in which various people (including bodybuilders) were given varying extra quantities of protein each day. Summing one study up, Dr. Richard Krieder from the University of Memphis said, "Although it is important for athletes to get an adequate amount of protein…consuming additional amounts of protein does not appear to promote muscle growth."

MYTH Fast food is bad for you.

BULLSHIT! A very wise man once said, "All things in moderation." This ancient phrase applies to most things in life—including fast food. A moderate amount of fast food is no worse for you than a moderate amount of home-cooked meat and vegetables. A constant diet of nothing but fast food may not be the healthiest choice you can make, but then again, eating macaroni and cheese every night is not very healthy either. Variety and moderation are the keys to good eating and health. If you feel like having a cheeseburger, eat one.

MYTH   Decaf is caffeine-free.

BULLSHIT!   International standards require decaf to be 97 percent caffeine free (EU standards are a little stricter at 99.9 percent). The process of removing caffeine is a long one that also eliminates many other chemicals (up to 400 in fact) that are essential to the taste of coffee. If you have an allergy to caffeine, you should probably keep away from all forms of coffee—decaf included. But for

those who can cope with caffeine (unless you really can't stand the slight "high" produced by it), you will have a nicer-tasting drink if you just opt for regular coffee. And if that doesn't convince you, the chemical often used in decaffeinating coffee beans (dichloromethane) is also used as a paint stripper.

MYTH   When we get cravings for certain foods, such as fruit juice, it is because our bodies lack a certain nutrient.

BULLSHIT!   Interestingly, scientists who put this to the test found out that it isn't true at all. In the study, a person who craved chocolate was given a cocktail of chemicals that contained all of the essential components (minus taste) of chocolate, and another cocktail containing chocolate flavor but no components of chocolate. The craving was satisfied when the person took the chocolate-flavored cocktail, but not when the essentially flavorless chocolate was consumed. This strongly suggests that cravings are simply emotional. We crave certain foods because of the memories and emotions relating to that food in our lives.

MYTH Mouton-Rothschild is a top-grade Chateau claret.

BULLSHIT! The five growths (classes) of red Bordeaux were determined in 1855. Four were considered First Class: Lafite-Rothschild, Latour, Margaux, and Haut-Brion. Mouton-Rothschild did not like being placed in second class, so their motto is "*Premier ne puis. Second ne daigne. Mouton suis.*" (First I cannot be. Second I do not deign to be. I am Mouton.) All I know is, I certainly would not turn down a glass of it.

MYTH Excess salt intake increases your blood pressure.

BULLSHIT! This is a myth that originated in the 1940s when a professor used salt reduction to treat people with high blood pressure. Science has since determined that there is no reason for a person with normal blood pressure to restrict their salt intake.

However, if you already have high blood pressure, you may become salt-sensitive, in which case you should reduce salt or increase your potassium intake as it is the balance of the two that really matters. Furthermore, people who suffer from hypertension should be careful with salt as it can have an impact. Ultimately, eating more potassium to decrease blood pressure is probably more important than reducing salt is. Potassium-rich foods include spinach, broccoli, bananas, white potatoes, and most types of beans.

MYTH Model T Fords only came out in black.

BULLSHIT! Model T Fords initially came out in a variety of colors—not just black. However, between 1914 and 1925 you could only buy one in black. It is also wrong that Ford said  that buyers could have a Model T in any color as long as it was black.

MYTH The Vikings were dirty, wild-looking, savage men and women.

BULLSHIT! In many movies and cartoons, this is how they are portrayed, but in reality, the Vikings were quite vain about their appearance. In fact, combs, tweezers, razors, and "ear spoons" are among some of the artifacts most frequently found in Viking Age excavations. These same excavations have also shown that the Vikings made soap. Vikings living in England even had a reputation for excessive cleanliness because of their custom of bathing once a week (on Saturday). To this day, Saturday is referred to as

MYTH The great Colossus of Rhodes stretched across the harbor of Rhodes.

BULLSHIT! We have all seen drawings of the great Colossus of Rhodes straddling the harbor of Rhodes—one leg on either side. This is not a true representation of how the statue appeared. It was standing with both legs together on one side of the harbor entrance.

laugardagur, laurdag, lørdag, and *lördag,* or "washing day" in the Scandinavian languages, though the original meaning is lost in modern speech in most cases. However, *laug* does still mean *bath* or *pool* in Icelandic.

MYTH Pirates walked the plank.

BULLSHIT! Pirates didn't walk the plank, nor did they make their captives walk the plank. When pirates wanted to dispose of someone, they did the most obvious and simple thing: They tossed them overboard.

MYTH The Middle Ages were splattered with the blood of those who died of the death penalty.

BULLSHIT! The Middle Ages gave birth to the jury system, and trials were in fact very fair. The death penalty was considered to be extremely severe and was used only in the worst cases of crimes like murder, treason, and arson. It was not until the Middle Ages began to draw to a close that rulers such as Elizabeth I began to use the death penalty as a means to rid their nations of religious opponents. Public beheadings were not as we see in the movies—they were performed only on the rich and were usually not done in public. The most common method of execution was hanging, and burning was extremely rare (and usually performed after the criminal had been hanged to death first).

MYTH Atia was a manipulative schemer.

BULLSHIT! HBO and the BBC created an excellent series called *Rome*, which dramatizes a number of years of the Roman Empire. In the series, however, they have unfortunately slandered the good name of Atia (mother of Octavian-Augustus, and niece of Julius Caesar). In the show she is seen as a licentious, self-absorbed, and manipulative schemer who is Mark Antony's lover. In reality, Atia was a highly moral woman, well regarded by Roman society at the time. Tacitus had this to say of her: "In her presence no base word could be uttered without grave offence, and no wrong deed done. Religiously and with the utmost delicacy she regulated not only the serious tasks of her youthful charges, but also their recreations and their games."

MYTH The Nazis made soap from humans.

BULLSHIT! The misconception that the Nazis made soap from humans is most likely attributable to the fact that they produced soap stamped with the letters "R. I. F." The soap was used in some concentration camps, and people mistakenly believed the letters stood for the German translation of "Pure Jewish Fat" in German, but it actually meant "Reich Industry Fat." Bars of this soap have been tested, and they contain no human DNA at all. The idea of soap made from human fat was also circulating in France during World War I.

MYTH   Independence Day in the U.S. commemorates July 4, 1776.

BULLSHIT!   It wasn't until seven years later that both the American and the British signed a peace agreement and King George III agreed to the independence—it takes two to tango. If the date of the signing of the Definitive Treaty of Peace were used as the date for the official U.S. holiday, Americans would celebrate Independence Day in commemoration of September 3, 1783.

MYTH   The Middle Ages were replete with starving peasants.

BULLSHIT!   In reality, peasants (manual laborers) would have had fresh porridge and bread daily—with beer to drink. In addition, each day they would have an assortment of dried or cured meats, cheeses, and fruits and vegetables from their area. Poultry, such as chicken, ducks, pigeons, and geese, was not uncommon on the peasants' dinner tables. Some peasants also liked to keep bees to provide honey. (Given the choice between McDonald's and medieval peasant food, I suspect the peasant food would be more nutritious and tasty.) The rich of the time had a great choice of meats, such as beef and lamb. They would eat more courses for each meal than the poor would, and would probably have had a number of spiced dishes—something the poor could not afford. Hollywood has a lot to answer for when it comes to spreading myths about the medieval period.

MYTH   Ancient Greece gave us democracy.

BULLSHIT!   Ancient Greece is not the name of a nation—it is the name of the region in which up to 1,000 individual cultures lived and worked alongside each other. Each culture had its own rulers, its own armies, its own independence from the others. We have heard of Sparta and the Spartans; that is just one of the multitude of different states within the Greek region. The people of all city-states were united by language and race, but wars among them was not at all uncommon, which is why the ancient Olympics were governed by a special rule guaranteeing protection to competitors traveling from their state to the host state.

MYTH Drinking alcohol was outlawed by the 18th Amendment (Prohibition).

BULLSHIT! Drinking alcohol was never outlawed—only making, transporting, and selling it were outlawed. Liquor could legally be consumed provided it was purchased before Prohibition. If you want to get technical about it, the 18th Amendment did not even outlaw manufacture, transport, or sale of alcohol; it was the Volstead Act that implemented Prohibition. The 21st Amendment would later repeal the 18th Amendment, but it would remain illegal to transport alcohol in areas where it was still banned (so-called dry counties).

MYTH   The Vikings were a part of one nation.

BULLSHIT!   Actually, the Vikings were different groups of warriors, explorers, and merchants led by a chieftain. During the Viking age, Scandinavia was not separated into Denmark, Norway, and Sweden as it is today. Instead, each chieftain ruled over a small area. The word *viking* does not refer to any location, but is the Old Norse word for a person participating in an expedition to sea.

MYTH   People starved to death during the Great Depression.

BULLSHIT!   When we think of the Great Depression, we picture hoards of families starving to death. Though it is true that there was hunger and malnutrition, virtually no one died of starvation. The resourcefulness of people at the time made it possible for them to find food in all sorts of places. Curiously, this also helped make rationing easier during World War II, because people had become used to living austerely.

MYTH   The former Soviet Union celebrated the October Revolution in October.

BULLSHIT!   Although the Bolsheviks took control during October 25 and 26, 1917, this was under the old style (Julian) calendar. One of the first things the communists did was to modernize their calendar to the Gregorian calendar, thereby pushing the day ahead 13 days (into November). This was a major holiday in the Soviet Union, mostly because the official ban on religion made the biggest holidays civil ones such as May Day and the October Revolution.

MYTH   All peasants had thatched-roof houses with animals living in them.

BULLSHIT!   First of all, the thatched roofs of medieval dwellings were woven into a tight mat—they were not just bundles of straw and sticks thrown on top of the house. Animals would not easily have been able to get inside the house through the roof. And considering how concerned about hygiene the average Middle Ager was, if an animal did get inside, it would be promptly removed—just as we remove birds or other small creatures that enter our homes today. Also, for the record, thatched roofs were not just for the poor; many castles and grander homes had them, too, because they worked so well. There are many homes in English villages today that still have thatched roofs.

MYTH   The Spanish flu came from Spain.

BULLSHIT!   Actually, the first cases showed up in the United States and the rest of Europe before hitting Spain. It is merely because Spain had very little news censorship at the time (compared to the other nations) that people got the impression that the disease was especially rampant there. So much for honesty being the best policy! The Spanish flu was a terrible pandemic that swept the world for two years, beginning in 1918. It is believed that some 50 to 100 million people perished as a result of the flu.

MYTH   Vikings drank from skull cups.

BULLSHIT!   The origin of this legend is from Ole Worm's *Reuner seu Danica literatura antiquissima* from 1636, in which he writes that Danish warriors drank from the "curved branches of skulls"—i.e., horns, which was probably mistranslated in Latin to mean "human skulls." The fact is, however, no skull cups have ever been found in excavations from the Viking Age.

MYTH   Medieval people took no baths and smelled awful.

BULLSHIT!   Not only is this a total myth, it is so widely believed that it has given rise to a whole other series of myths, such as the false belief that Church incense was designed to hide the stink of so many people in one place. In fact, the incense was part of the Church's rituals because of Christianity's history stemming from Judaism. The Jewish religion also used incense in its sacrifices. This myth has also lead to the strange idea that people usually married in May or June because they didn't stink so badly having had their yearly bath. This is, of course, a total myth as well. People married in those months because marriage was not allowed during Lent (the season of penance). So, back to smelly people. In the Middle Ages, most towns had bathhouses. In fact, cleanliness and hygiene were very highly regarded—so much so that bathing was incorporated into various ceremonies, such as those surrounding knighthood. Some people bathed daily, others less regularly, but most people did bathe. Furthermore, they used hot water; they just had to heat it up themselves, unlike us with our modern plumbing. The French put it best in the following Latin statement: *Venari, ludere, lavari, bibere; hoc est vivere*! To hunt, to play, to wash, to drink; this is to live!

MYTH Vikings used crude, unsophisticated weapons such as clubs and axes.

BULLSHIT! The Vikings were actually skilled weapon smiths. Using a method called pattern welding, the Vikings could make swords that were both extremely sharp and flexible. According to the Viking sagas, one method of testing these weapons was to place the sword hilt first in a cold stream and float a hair down to it. If it cut the hair, it was considered a good sword.

MYTH Amazon women warriors had one breast.

BULLSHIT! When it comes to myths, they don't often date back as far as this one. In the 5th century BC the ancient Greek Hellanicus heard of the Amazon women and thought the word was derived from *a* (without) and *mastos* (breast). Consequently, he decided that the Amazon women warriors must have one breast, the other having been cut off to facilitate the use of a bow and arrow. Ridiculous, but this notion really did stay around for a long time.

MYTH   The emperor gave a thumbs up or down as a signal for a gladiator to kill his enemy.

BULLSHIT!   The emperor (and only the emperor) would give an open or closed hand. If his palm was flat, it meant "spare his life"; if it was closed, it meant "kill him." If a gladiator killed his opponent before the emperor gave his permission, the gladiator would be put on trial for murder, as only the emperor had the right to condemn a man to death.

MYTH The Romans spoke classical Latin.

BULLSHIT! The Romans spoke a form of Latin known as vulgar Latin, it quite different from the classical Latin that we generally think of them speaking (classical Latin is what we usually learn in school). Vulgar Latin is the language that the Romance languages (Italian, French, etc.) developed from. Classical Latin was used as an official language only. In addition, members of the Eastern Roman Empire were speaking Greek exclusively by the 4th century, and Greek had replaced Latin as the official language.

MYTH Vikings were big, bulging guys with long blond hair.

BULLSHIT! Historical records show that the average Viking man was about 5 feet, 7 inches tall, which was not especially tall for the time. Blond hair was seen as ideal in the Viking culture, and many Nordic men bleached their hair with a special soap. But many people who had been kidnapped as slaves became part of the Viking population in time. So, in Viking groups, you would probably find Italians, Spaniards, Portuguese, French, and Russians—a very diverse group built around a core of Vikings from a particular region, which resulted in a range of physical appearances.

MYTH   All peasants did in the Middle Ages was backbreaking work.

BULLSHIT!   While peasants in the Middle Ages did work hard (tilling the fields was the only way to ensure you could eat), they had regular festivals (religious and secular), which involved dancing, drinking, games, and tournaments. Many of the games of the time are still played today: chess, checkers, dice, blindman's bluff, and many more. It may not seem like these activities would have been as much fun as the latest video games are now, but it was a great opportunity to enjoy the especially warm weather that was caused by the Medieval Warm Period.

MYTH   The Romans feasted until they were full and then regurgitated their food in the vomitorium so they could start over again.

BULLSHIT!   Actually, the vomitoria were passages that enabled people to move quickly to and from their seats in an amphitheater. These vomitoria made it possible for thousands of Roman citizens to be seated within minutes.

MYTH   Robert Fulton's famous steamship was named the *Clermont*.

BULLSHIT!   All of the official records list the boat as *North River Steam Boat*, and even Fulton called it the *North River*. A later biographer accidentally called it the *Clermont*, which was the city where it was berthed. There were other steamboats before the *North River*, but like many inventors, Fulton is given credit because he made the first practical one. His boat ferried passengers on the New York City–Albany run and usually took all day, including an overnight stop. A side note: The engine for the *North River* was built by another famous inventor who took an existing idea and made it practical–James Watt.

Also, Fulton built a working submarine and called it the *Nautilus*.

MYTH Issac Newton devised his universal law of gravity when an apple fell from a tree onto his head.

BULLSHIT! It's always exciting to think of a great discovery happening in the blink of an eye—we imagine that if it were not for the right person being in the right place at the right time, man would have lost an incredibly significant piece of knowledge. For this reason, people have clung to the idea that Newton

MYTH The term *plebeian* refered to the common or poorer classes.

BULLSHIT! In Rome, a plebeian was just a member of the general populace of Rome (as opposed to the patricians, who were the privileged classes). Plebeians could, and very often did, become very wealthy people—but wealth did not change their class.

devised his universal law of gravity because of an apple hitting him on the head. But in fact the first mention of an apple in relation to Newton came 60 years after his death in 1727: "Whilst he was musing in a garden it came into his thought that the power of gravity (which brought an apple from the tree to the ground) was not limited to a certain distance from the earth but that this power must extend much further." (John Conduitt)

MYTH   Caesar's last words were "*Et tu, Brute*" ("And you Brutus").

BULLSHIT!   Caesar's last words were actually "And you also," as recorded (in Greek) by Suetonius: Και συ Τέκνον (*kai su teknon*). These words were spoken to Brutus, which is undoubtedly the reason that Shakespeare coined the phrase, "Et tu, Brute?" The meaning of his last words is unknown—but it would seem fair to think that he was telling his murderer, "You will be next." Caesar was bilingual (Greek and Latin) and Greek was the dominant language in Rome at the time, so it is not unreasonable that his last words would have been uttered in that language and not Latin as is commonly believed.

MYTH   The Middle Ages were an extremely violent time.

BULLSHIT!   Though there was violence in the Middle Ages (just as there had always been), there were no equals to the more modern terror of Stalin, Hitler, and Mao. Most people lived their lives without experiencing violence. The Inquisition was not the violent bloodlust that many movies and books have claimed it to be, and most modern historians now admit this readily. Modern times have seen genocide, mass murder, and serial killing—something virtually unheard of before the Enlightenment. In fact, there are really only two serial killers of note from the Middle Ages: Elizabeth Bathory and Gilles de Rais.

MYTH   The Vikings lived only in Scandinavia.

BULLSHIT!   The Vikings did originate from the Scandinavian countries, but over time they started settlements in many places, reaching as far as North Africa, Russia, Constantinople, and even North America. There are a variety of theories about the motives driving the Viking expansion, the most common of which is that the Scandinavian population had outgrown the agricultural potential of their

MYTH   All Roman men wore togas.

BULLSHIT!   Actually, the toga was a very formal piece of clothing. To say that the Romans always wore togas would be the same as saying that the English always wear top hats and tails. Juvenal says this: "There are many parts of Italy, to tell the truth, in which no man puts on a toga until he is dead." Average Romans would have worn tunics.

homeland. Another theory is that the old trade routes of Western Europe and Eurasia experienced a decline in profitability when the Roman Empire fell in the 5th century, forcing the Vikings to open new trading routes in order to profit from international trade.

One could imagine that the Vikings were hated everywhere because of their raids, but it seems that they were also respected by some. The French King Charles III—known as Charles the Simple—gave the Vikings the land they had already settled on in France

(Normandy), and he even gave his daughter to the Viking chief Rollo. In return, the Vikings protected France against wilder Vikings. Also, in Constantinople the Vikings were acknowledged for their strength—so much so that the Varangian guard of the Byzantine emperors in the 11th century was made up entirely of Swedish Vikings.

MYTH   Christopher Columbus discovered that the world was round.

BULLSHIT!   Surprisingly, this old myth is believed by millions of people. What we are told is that peers of Columbus doomed his trip to failure because they thought he would fall off the edge of the earth. Now, this was in the 1490s, but man has known the earth was round since the idea was first put forth by Pythagorus 2,000 years earlier. Columbus did fail to reach his original destination, and in so doing he "discovered" the Americas. Not a bad end to a failed journey. However, the round-earth theory was so well established by that time that his navigational methods were all based on the fact that the earth was round.

MYTH Women in the Middle Ages were oppressed.

BULLSHIT! In the 1960s and 1970s, this idea flourished. In fact, all we need to do is think of a few significant women from the period to see that this is not true at all: St. Joan of Arc was a young woman who was given full control of the French army! Her downfall was political and would have occurred whether she were male or female. Hildegard von Bingen was a polymath in the Middle Ages who was held in such high esteem that kings, popes, and lords all sought her advice. Her music and writing exists to this day. Elizabeth I ruled as a powerful queen in her own right, and many other nations had women leaders. Granted, women did not work on cathedrals, but they certainly pulled their weight in the fields and villages. Furthermore, the rules of chivalry meant that women had to

be treated with the greatest of dignity. The biggest difference between the concept of feminism in the Middle Ages and now is that in the Middle Ages it was believed that women were "equal in dignity, different in function"; now the concept has been modified to "equal in dignity and function."

MYTH   The Viking raids were very violent.

BULLSHIT!   It was a violent age, and the question is whether non-Viking armies were any less bloodthirsty and barbaric. For instance, Charlemagne, who was the Vikings' contemporary, virtually exterminated the whole people of Avars. At Verden, he ordered the beheading of 4,500 Saxons. What really made the Vikings different was the fact that they seemed to take special care to destroy items of religious value (Christian monasteries and holy sites) and kill churchmen, which earned them quite a bit of hatred in a highly religious time. The Vikings probably enjoyed the reputation they had; people were so scared of them that they often fled from their cities instead of defending them when they saw a Viking ship coming near.

MYTH When the Romans conquered Carthage, they salted the farmlands to prevent anything from growing.

BULLSHIT! In fact, this is a 20th-century myth with no bearing in reality. When the Romans conquered Carthage, they went from house to house capturing slaves and slaughtering the rest. They burned the city to the ground and left it as a pile of ruins. This resulted in the loss of a great deal of historical information on Carthage, which makes the study of it difficult in modern times.

MYTH The Titanic was the first ship to send out the SOS signal.

BULLSHIT! Initially, the Titanic sent out the CQD signal (standing for "All stations: distress"), but Britain had recently signed up to the new standard of SOS, so one of the crew suggested that it be used as well; "Send SOS; it's the new call, and besides, this may be your last chance to send it!" It certainly was new to British ships, but the standard had been in use for some years prior and there is even a newspaper article from 1909 that describes its use by an American ship, the *Arapahoe*.

MYTH   All Roman men were gladiators.

BULLSHIT!   We think of gladiators as having been male, but in fact, women were gladiators too (though they were called gladiatrices—or gladiatrix for singular). Though the first documented appearance of gladiatrices appears under the reign of Nero (AD 37 to 68), there are implications in earlier documents that suggest they existed before. A strong condemnation against female gladiators of the Flavian and Trajanic eras can be found in the Satire VI of Juvenal, decrying the fact female gladiators were typically from upper-class families and were seeking thrills and attention. Emperor Severus banned female gladiators around AD 200, but records show that this ban was largely ignored.

MYTH   Witches were burned in Salem.

BULLSHIT!   In the terrible miscarriage of justice that took place in 1692, 20 people (14 women and 6 men) were executed; but of those 20 all but one were hanged. The one man who wasn't hanged, Giles Corey, died in the middle of "judicial" torture—he was crushed to death under heavy stones.

MYTH   The Great Fire of London in 1666 ended the Great Plague of 1665.

BULLSHIT!   A study done by the University of London recently found no correlation between the location of the fire and the geography of the dreadful plague. It was just a coincidence that the fire happened around the same time as the plague was beginning to mysteriously disappear. Most of the areas

affected by the plague were poor parts of London—
north, south, and east of the city walls—whereas the
fire was in the city itself. *Encyclopaedia Britannica*
says, "The cessation of plague in England must be
regarded as spontaneous."

MYTH　All Vikings were warriors.

BULLSHIT!　While we all imagine the Vikings
living from the spoils of sacking and pillaging, only a
very small percentage of the Vikings were warriors;
the majority were farmers, craftsmen, and traders. For
the Vikings who took to the sea, pillaging was just one
among many goals of their expeditions. The Vikings
settled peacefully in many places such as Iceland and
Greenland, and were international merchants of their
time; they peacefully traded with almost every county
of the then-known world.

MYTH　Slaves built the pyramids in Egypt.

BULLSHIT!　How many of us have been tricked
by Hollywood into thinking that slaves built the
pyramids? Most of us, probably. The pyramids were
actually built by local Egyptians in the permanent
employ of the pharaoh. And it appears that they

liked their jobs, as grafitti shows that they worked in competitive groups that had fun names like "Friends of Khufu" and "Drunkards of Menkaure." So, the pyramids were built on the back of a bit of friendly rivalry, not backbreaking slave labor.

MYTH   People in the Middle Ages believed the Earth was flat.

BULLSHIT!   No one since the ancient Greeks believed the Earth to be flat. Furthermore, people did not believe the Earth was the center of the universe. The famous monk Copernicus dealt a death blow to that idea (without being punished) well before Galileo was tried for heresy for claiming that it proved the

Bible was wrong. Science historians David Lindberg and Ronald Numbers recently published *God and Nature*, a book in which they say, "There was scarcely a Christian scholar of the Middle Ages who did not acknowledge [Earth's] sphericity and even know its approximate circumference."

MYTH   Abraham Lincoln's Emancipation Proclamation abolished slavery.

BULLSHIT!   The Emancipation Proclamation (1862) declared the freedom of all slaves in the confederate states—that is, the states over which Lincoln and the Union government had no control. Furthermore, it did not free slaves from any of the states that were already under Union control. This would be (in a sense) like Australians trying to declare a binding law on New Zealanders when they are two separate nations. The Emancipation Proclamation was, effectively, worthless. It was not until the 13th Amendment (December 6, 1865), that slavery was officially abolished in full.

MYTH   Classical Roman statues and buildings were finished in white stone or marble.

BULLSHIT! When most of us think of the Romans and Greeks, we think of the beautiful white statues and buildings that they left behind. But even way back in the 1800s, statues that had been excavated were found to contain traces of paint pigment. At the time,

color was considered a non-essential part of beauty, so no one bothered to try to replicate the original appearance of these great works of art. Fortunately for us, in more recent years people have tried to replicate the original appearance of these sculptures by matching the pigments found embedded in the stone.

MYTH The Middle Ages were full of religious superstition and ignorance.

BULLSHIT! Leading historians deny that there is any evidence of this. Science and philosophy blossomed at the time—partly due to the introduction of universities all over Europe. The Middle Ages produced some of the greatest art, music, and literature in all history. Boethius, Boccaccio, Dante, Petrarch, and Machiavelli are still revered today for their brilliant minds. The cathedrals and castles of Europe are still standing and contain some of the most beautiful artwork and stonework man has been able to create with his bare hands. Medicine at the time was primitive, but it was structured and willing to embrace new ideas when they arose (which is why we now have modern medicine).

MYTH   American colonists protested the tea tax with the Boston Tea Party because of an increase in the price of tea.

BULLSHIT!   The American colonists preferred Dutch tea to English tea. The English Parliament placed an embargo on Dutch tea in the colonies, so a huge smuggling operation developed. To combat this, the English government lowered the tax on tea so that the English tea would be price-competitive with Dutch teas. The colonists (actually, some colonists led by the chief smugglers) protested by dumping the tea into Boston Harbor.

MYTH   The Vikings wore horned helmets.

BULLSHIT!   There are no records of such helmets having ever existed. All depictions of Viking helmets dating to the Viking age, show helmets with no horns, and the only authentic Viking helmet that has ever been found does not have them either. An explanation for the helmet-with-horns myth is that Christians in contemporary Europe added the detail to make the Vikings look even more barbaric and pagan, with horns like Satan's on their heads. It should be noted that the Norse god Thor is depicted wearing a helmet with wings on it, which do look somewhat similar to horns.

MYTH   Dinosaurs and humans coexisted.

BULLSHIT!   In recent years, perhaps due to religious sentiments, many people have come to believe that dinosaurs and humans lived alongside each other. In reality, the last dinosaurs (aside from birds) died out in a dramatic fashion nearly 65 million years ago, while humans have been walking the earth for a mere 6 million years.

MYTH   Neanderthals couldn't speak like humans because they only had a basic capacity for sound in their throats.

BULLSHIT!   In 1983, in a cave in Israel, scientists found a Neanderthal hyoid bone (part of the vocal mechanism) that was identical to that of modern humans. This means that Neanderthals' capacity for speech (at least physically) is the same as our own. There is no reason to believe that they did not have at least a basic system of vocal communication.

MYTH Toilet water spins counterclockwise in the Northern Hemisphere and clockwise in the Southern Hemisphere.

BULLSHIT! That phenomenon only occurs in weather patterns of hundreds of miles in size like hurricanes, due to the rotation of the Earth.

MYTH The sound you hear when you snap your fingers is from your thumb rubbing against your middle finger.

BULLSHIT! The sound you hear is actually your middle finger hitting the base of your thumb.

MYTH Humans use only 10 percent of their brains.

BULLSHIT! This is utterly false. No one really knows how this myth started, but we do know how it has been perpetuated for so long. When people first began making this false claim, psychics decided that this explained why some people had paranormal abilities and others didn't: Paranormal powers were unleashed in people who had developed the use of more than 10 percent of the brain. They believed that some region of the brain, if tapped, could provide psychic abilities. This certainly helped their bottom line, as thousands of books have since come out aiming to "teach" people how to develop this power. So, the truth of the matter? Humans use 100 percent of their brains—that is why it is there! Here is a case in point: a hemispherectomy, the surgical procedure that removes an entire half of the brain. When this surgery is performed, the patient becomes paralyzed in half of their body.

MYTH   We have five body senses—sight, hearing, touch, smell, and taste.

BULLSHIT!   These are the traditional five senses, but there are in fact many more—some say up to 21. Obvious additions to the list are balance, pain, and temperature. Furthermore, we have internal senses, which traditionally number four: imagination, memory, common sense, and the estimative power.

MYTH   Neanderthals exclusively used clubs as weapons.

BULLSHIT!   Neanderthals actually had many highly developed tools and weapons—such as spears for killing mammoths, and stone tools. They are thought to have used tools of the Mousterian class, which were often produced using soft hammer percussion, with hammers made of materials like bones, antlers, and wood (as opposed to the hard hammer percussion produced by stone hammers). Many of these tools were very sharp. There is also good evidence that they used a lot of wooden objects, which are unlikely to have been preserved until today.

MYTH   Fifty percent or more of all humans ever born are alive today.

BULLSHIT!   This myth was probably perpetuated by eugenicists and other people who believe the planet should be saved by population control of the human species. This is not a new myth either: In 1798, Thomas Malthus predicted that population growth would surpass the world food supply by the mid 1800s. The Population Reference Bureau estimates that the earth has held more than 106 billion humans throughout history. With a current world population of more than 6 billion, that means that roughly 6 percent of people ever born are alive today—a significantly lower number than that given by population explosion alarmists. What is perhaps more frightening is the fact that many nations today are not producing enough children to replace the population with no growth at all. In other words, many countries are suffering negative birthrates.

MYTH   Humans are descended from Neanderthals.

MYTH The North Pole is "north" and the South Pole is "south."

BULLSHIT! BS, technically speaking. In terms of physics, the North Pole (though geographically in the north) is actually a south magnetic pole, and the South Pole (geographically in the south) is a north magnetic pole. When your compass is pointing north, it is actually pointing to the south pole of earth's magnetic field. About 780,000 years ago, this would not have been the case, as the magnetic poles of the earth were reversed (this is called a geomagnetic reversal). Oh, and just to complicate things further, the poles drift around randomly—they are not in a fixed spot. This is most likely due to movements in the molten nickel-iron alloy in the earth's core.

BULLSHIT! Actually, Neanderthals and modern men existed side by side as two separate groups. Recent DNA studies have found that the Neanderthals are a distinct evolutionary line—a line that was ultimately a dead end, as they all died out around 30,000 years ago. The extinction of Neanderthals was most likely caused by slightly lower birthrates and higher mortality rates, combined with an increasingly unstable climate.

MYTH   Mammals arrived after the dinosaurs became extinct, giving them a safe haven to develop and survive.

BULLSHIT!   The reality is quite different. Both dinosaurs and mammals (synapsids) lived together quite happily. In fact, the genetic line of the synapsids predates and postdates the dinosaurs.

MYTH   Mirrors reverse left and right.

BULLSHIT!   When we look in a mirror, our left and right sides appear to be reversed—left is right and right is left. In fact, what has really happened is that the mirror has inverted us front and back. The reason that we think it is a left-to-right reversal is that we are used to a person's left and right being reversed when they turn to face us. So what is the mirror doing? Imagine a person with his back to us doing a handstand to face us, rather than turning around. His right and left remain the same, but his top and bottom swap. Looking into a mirror has the same effect: nothing reverses in the mirror—not bottom and top, not left and right.

MYTH   Most rocket launches in the U.S. happen at Cape Canaveral.

BULLSHIT!   Most of them are launched from

Merritt Island in Brevard County, Florida, where NASA's JFK Space Center is located. All shuttle launches have occurred, at Merritt Island, whereas only a small number of rockets were launched from the now decommissioned Launch Complex in Cape Canaveral. The last manned spaceflight from Cape Canaveral took off more than 30 years ago.

MYTH   Glass is a very slow-flowing liquid.

BULLSHIT!   The reason many people believe this is due to the nature of old panes of glass in which the bottom appears to be thicker than the top, suggesting that the glass is "melting" and pooling at the bottom. This distortion in the glass is the result of past manufacturing methods. You will notice that you don't see this "melting" behavior in modern glass windows. Glass is actually an amorphous ceramic.

MYTH   An asteroid wiped out the dinosaurs.

BULLSHIT!   An asteroid impact didn't kill off the dinosaurs. Though it is true that there was a massive impact 65 million years ago, there is no proof at all that it killed all the dinosaurs; there is every chance that many survived. The asteroid would most certainly have killed any dinosaurs in the vicinity, but not the entire planet's worth. The impact did most likely affect weather patterns, though, and these may have also contributed to the demise of dinosaurs in faraway places.

MYTH   Alexander Graham Bell invented the telephone.

BULLSHIT!   Ask anyone, "Who invented the telephone?" and they will tell you: Alexander Graham Bell. We have all heard the tale of Mr. Bell inventing the phone and using it for the first time to call his secretary, Mr. Watson, but the first functioning telephone was actually invented 15 years earlier by Philipp Reis, a German inventor. His device (which he called the Reis Telephon) was first demonstrated in 1861. The Reis Telephon was able to transmit musical tones quite clearly but human voices only faintly. There is no doubt at all that the first transmission of human voices over wire was on the device created by Reis, a full 15 years prior to the invention by the man who now receives all the credit for it.

MYTH   *Aluminium* is an older term than *aluminum.*

BULLSHIT!   Most Americans may not be familiar with this myth but it is very widespread outside the U.S.: *Aluminum* is actually the older term, while *aluminium* was created later by the British to make it sound more like the other elements. Here is a timeline

MYTH Copernicus was the first person to state that the earth revolves around the sun.

BULLSHIT! That theory was first taught by unknown ancient thinkers. While we don't know their names, we do know for certain that, from as early as the 7th century BC, the revolution of the earth around the sun was mentioned in Sanskrit documents.

that explains things clearly. 1808: Sir Humphrey Davy isolates the metal for the first time. He calls it alumium. 1812: Sir Humphrey decides to change the spelling of his element; he renames it aluminum, the term adopted in the United States. 1812: British scientists dislike the new name and change it to aluminium to match the other classical-sounding elements. So, if we are to give the discoverer the naming rights, the proper term is aluminum. And for those who love grammar, here is an off-topic aside: from the late 17th century, *fall* was the universal English word for the third season (both British and Americans used it exclusively). It was not until the 18th century that the British began to use the very old-fashioned (dating from the 14th century) word *autumn*, while the Americans continued to use *fall*.

MYTH   There were marine and avian dinosaurs.

BULLSHIT!   All dinosaurs were land dwellers. None of the marine reptiles (such as plesiosaurs) were dinosaurs. Some marine creatures, like the crocodile, were definitely related to the dinosaur but weren't true dinosaurs. This is also true of the flying reptiles such as pterosaurs.

MYTH   "Letting it out" alleviates anger.

BULLSHIT!   This a very common myth about psychology in which people believe they will alleviate their anger by "letting it out." This is such a popular concept that many therapies have grown up around it, utilizing tools like punching bags, squeeze balls, etc. In fact, the opposite is found to be true. When a person expresses anger regularly, it becomes habit-forming. Though an individual may experience temporary relief

from anger after smashing a plate against a wall, ultimately fits of anger will become an addiction and the person will begin to seek out more reasons to become angry, in order to achieve that nice feeling. So ultimately, the best thing to do: Bottle it up!

MYTH   The rainbow is seven colors: red, orange, yellow, green, blue, indigo, and violet.

BULLSHIT!   We are, no doubt, all familiar with the old phrase "Roy G. Biv," used to remember the seven colors of the rainbow: red, orange, yellow, green, blue, indigo, violet. This series of colors was coined by Isaac Newton, who initially excluded indigo and violet. Although a rainbow does appear to have seven colors, it is in fact one continuous spectrum of color, and it is merely an artifact of human color perception that makes it appear to be a series of bands. There are also things called supernumerary rainbows, which have more than seven bands visible to the human eye.

MYTH   Neanderthals walked with constantly bent knees like a monkey.

BULLSHIT!   This is one of those very unfortunate cases of a discovery leading to much confusion: a skeleton of a Neanderthal that had bent knees was discovered at the start of the 20th century, giving rise to the popular belief that all Neanderthals did. In fact, it turns out the skeleton was of a

MYTH There is a dark side of the moon.

BULLSHIT! We have all heard of the dark side of the moon, which often makes us presume that the moon is stationary, but in fact the moon rotates just as earth does—once for each orbit (to the observer). And, incidentally, the dark side of the moon is actually just the night side; it is no more a fixed feature of the moon than the night side of the earth.

Neanderthal that suffered from arthritis. Neanderthals walked upright in the same manner as modern humans; they were generally only 5 to 6 inches shorter than modern humans, contrary to a common view of them as "very short" or "just over 5 feet."

MYTH A lot of small earthquakes help to alleviate the pressures building up that can cause a big one.

BULLSHIT!   Seismologists have observed that for every magnitude 6 earthquake, there are 10 of magnitude 5, 100 of magnitude 4, 1,000 of magnitude 3, and so forth as the events get smaller and smaller. This sounds like a lot of small earthquakes, but there are never enough small ones to eliminate the occasional large event. It would take 32 magnitude 5s, 1,000 magnitude 4s, and 32,000 magnitude 3s to equal the energy of one magnitude 6 event. So, even though we always record many more small events than large ones, there are never enough to eliminate the need for the occasional large earthquake.

MYTH   The stegasaurus dragged its tail.

BULLSHIT!   We all know stegosaurus as that heavy, small-headed dinosaur with an arched back and a dragging tail, sporting four spikes that pointed upward. Popular books always brought up the fact that stegosaurus had a brain the size of a walnut and that it was probably a very dumb animal that became extinct because it couldn't compete with the much better armored (and slightly smarter) ankylosaurs. However, our knowledge of stegosaurus, like many dinosaurs, has changed a lot since. Fossil footprints and detailed studies of its anatomy have proven that stegosaurus didn't drag its tail in the mud, but actually walked erect, like an elephant, with its tail held horizontally, parallel to the ground. Its back wasn't as arched as they had us believe, and the neck was not carried horizontally as usually depicted, but upright, like a bird's.

MYTH The Great Wall of China is the only man-made structure visible from space.

BULLSHIT! This is wrong on many levels. First, while you are still close enough to earth to actually see

the Great Wall, you can also see road networks and other large objects created by man. There is, in fact, no distance from earth at which you can only see the Great Wall. By the time you get a few thousand miles away, you can see nothing man-made. Astronaut Alan Bean said, "The only thing you can see from the moon is a beautiful sphere, mostly white [clouds], some blue [ocean], patches of yellow [deserts], and every once in a while some green vegetation. No man-made object is visible on this scale. In fact, when first leaving earth's orbit and only a few thousand miles away, no man-made object is visible at that point either."

MYTH   Neanderthals were savages.

BULLSHIT!   There is actually much evidence to show that Neanderthals cared for the sick and old in their communities. There has been fossil evidence that shows potentially life-threatening injuries that were completely healed, indicating that the Neanderthal who suffered the injuries was nursed back to health by another member of his group. There is also evidence (via fossilized musical instruments) that Neanderthals enjoyed and played music.

MYTH The "face" on Mars is an alien creation.

BULLSHIT! We have all seen the "face" on Mars and, despite much evidence to the contrary, many people still believe it is an alien creation. In the most recent fly-by of Mars, NASA was able to get a much clearer picture. Those who still believe that it is a nonnatural made hill are suffering from pareidolia.

MYTH There are questions about the physical attributes of Neanderthals that we will never be able to answer.

BULLSHIT! As of 2009, the complete Neanderthal genome has been mapped. The most important implication of this is that now it is technically possible to clone a Neanderthal—to raise them back from the dead so to speak. The current estimated cost of doing this is $30 million, and no one is putting up the cash. Ethical questions will always be raised regarding cloning, and this is also a hindrance. But there is absolutely no reason not to believe that we will—one day—be able to give birth to and raise a Neanderthal (or at least the closest thing possible to one).

MYTH   Wait 30 minutes after eating before you swim.

BULLSHIT!   Do you wait 30 minutes after eating before swimming? You don't have to! Although there

is a theoretical concern based on the fact that the body diverts the circulation of blood to the gut and away from the muscles, which might possibly cause a cramp, no one has ever drowned because they went swimming with a full tummy. Going swimming after eating a big meal might make you uncomfortable, but it won't cause you to drown. And even if you did get a cramp, in most cases you could easily exit the water before any real damage is done.

MYTH   Mercury is the hottest planet.

BULLSHIT!   Mercury is the closest planet to the sun but, despite this, it is not the hottest. The planet with the highest mean surface temperature is actually Venus, a consequence of its mostly carbon-dioxide atmosphere.

MYTH   NASA invented the Dustbuster.

BULLSHIT!   First of all, how do you vacuum in a vacuum? You don't, so why would NASA need a vacuum cleaner for its space missions? It didn't, but what it did need was a small battery-powered drill. So they teamed up with Black & Decker to come up with the perfect device. Once the device had been developed, Black & Decker was left with great technology from which they eventually developed the Dustbuster and other useful home devices.

MYTH   Cell phone use on a plane creates a risk of a crash.

BULLSHIT!   The FAA has tested all sorts of electronic devices for 25 years, at 100 times the RF (Radio Frequency) interference levels—and nothing happened. The FAA simply states that no link between operating the devices has been proved. It's been left up to the airlines to determine their own policy, and that policy is generally to put away your Blackberry. By using your cell phone during flight, you risk interfering with a flight crew, but the plane won't crash. Consequently, some airlines are now allowing the use of cell phones during flights.

MYTH   Sauropods were huge, clumsy denizens of the swamps, spending most of their time underwater feeding on aquatic plants.

BULLSHIT!   Diplodocus and its close relative apatosaurus (formerly known as brontosaurus) are

MYTH If you stand in the bottom of a deep well in broad daylight, you can see the stars.

BULLSHIT! This is an ancient myth mentioned by Aristotle. Logically thinking, the farther down a well you are, the smaller the top of the well appears, and consequently the darkness of the walls combines with that to make the opening appear dazzlingly bright—but not dark as it would need to be to see the stars.

among the best known sauropods, or giant long-necked dinosaurs. Or at least, they used to be well-known to the public; today, they look very different from the classic "brontosaurus" we knew. Sauropods' huge weight (up to 50 tons or more) was said to be too much for the creatures to move properly on land. Today, however, we know that sauropods didn't live in swamps. Actually, it seems that most species avoided swampy areas and preferred dry land environments. They had legs shaped like columns, and some of them didn't have toes at all; their legs looked like stumps or like tree trunks, and were exclusively adapted to support their massive weight. It turns out diplodocus and apatosaurus looked more like weird, dragonlike creatures than the smooth-skinned giants of *The Land Before Time* or *The Flintstones*. Their backs were adorned with sharp keratin blades, similar to those of a modern day iguana, and their skin was covered with bumpy scales and knobs.

MYTH Neanderthals had faces like apes.

BULLSHIT! This misconception came about through poor reconstructions from largely arthritic skeletons. In 1983, Jay Matternes (a forensic artist who did much work in fleshing out skulls for homicide investigations) performed a reconstruction on a much better specimen than had been seen before. The result was a face that is surprisingly similar to a normal male human face.

MYTH   There is a universal scientific method.

BULLSHIT!   Most of us were educated using elementary-level science books, which wrongly imply this for the sake of simplicity. But many sciences don't fit into the mold of the "scientific method" (most commonly defined as developing a hypothesis, conducting an experiment, and developing a conclusion). For example, astronomy: How does one experiment with black holes when we can't get near one? An enormous amount of our modern scientific knowledge has come from the result of curiosity and unguided research, such as cosmic microwave background radiation. Although the scientific method is definitely useful in basic physics and chemistry, real science encompasses many methods (or none, as we just mentioned).

MYTH   Neanderthals were all one race.

BULLSHIT!   Because we use one term to describe all Neanderthals, we tend to think of them as a single group of people sharing identical traits and features, but it is most likely that there were different ethnicities among Neanderthals, just as in humans. A recent study has determined that there were probably three racial groups within the Neanderthal family: "The conclusions of this study are consistent with existing paleoanthropological research and show that Neanderthals can be divided into at least three groups: one in western Europe, a second in the southern area, and a third in western Asia." [from "Genetic Evidence of Geographical Groups among Neanderthals" by Virginie Fabre, Silvana Condemi, and Anna Degioanni]

MYTH   Working out at a slower pace burns more calories from fat than a high-intensity workout does.

BULLSHIT!   We live in lazy times, and this misconception gives us a great excuse to put in minimal effort at the gym while feeling like we are achieving great things. It is true that you will burn a

MYTH   NASA spent millions of dollars trying to develop a pen to write in space when astronauts could just have used pencils.

BULLSHIT!   At first, astronauts did use pencils, but when a smart man developed a pressurized pen that not only would work in space, but also under the ocean as well, NASA purchased 400 of the pens at the cost of $6 per pen. The Soviets also bought his pens. To this day, both nations still use the Fisher Space Pen (named after its inventor, Paul Fisher).

greater percentage of fat in a low-intensity workout, but you burn more calories from fat in a high-intensity workout of the same duration. Confusing? In a low-intensity workout, you might burn 200 calories—of which 60 percent (120 calories) are from fat; but a high-intensity workout of the same duration might burn 400 calories (35 percent from fat, or 140 calories). This shows that it is obviously better to do the high-intensity training because not only do you burn more calories but you also get a much better cardiovascular workout.

MYTH   Archaeopteryx was a bird.

BULLSHIT!   Often called "the first bird," archaeopteryx is one of those creatures you could find in any book on dinosaurs or evolution. Often considered to be a sort of missing link between reptiles and birds, archaeopteryx has been used as a mascot both by scientists trying to prove evolution and creationists trying to disprove it (by claiming that archaeopteryx is simply a bird). However, the fossil evidence shows that both scientists and creationists were wrong. As more and more feathered dinosaurs are found in China—some of them even more similar to birds than the archaeopteryx was—it becomes obvious that this creature was not the missing link, and was not a bird at all.

MYTH Crimes and accidents increase in number during a full moon.

BULLSHIT! While it is almost impossible to debunk such a myth, there are no statistics relating to the incidence of crimes that supports this wacky theory.

MYTH Phone came before fax.

BULLSHIT! I can't tell you whether the chicken or the egg came first, but I can tell you that contrary to popular belief, the fax machine was invented before the telephone. Scottish inventor Alexander Bain had invented the electric clock back in 1841. In 1843 he used his work on the electric clock to patent a device that could be synchronized with a twin over telegraph lines, which, according to some stories, he did so that he could transmit a picture of a newborn calf. (If this is true, he would have needed the photo to be a daguerreotype, which seems very unlikely for just a cow.) Frederick Bakewell patented a better fax machine in 1848, two years before Bain updated his, and in 1861 an Italian named Giovanni Caselli invented the first high-quality fax. All of this was done before both Alexander Bell and Elisha Gray independently filed for the telephone patent on February 14, 1876.

MYTH   Neanderthals all lived in caves.

BULLSHIT!   This is partly true—some Neanderthals did live in caves (hence the term *cavemen*), but many of them lived in huts: "Winter homes were Ice Age huts, built teepee style, from branches and mammoth bones, covered with animal skins. These huts were used for many years, so they built them carefully. Holes were dug, deeply into the ground. Poles were inserted into these holes and then tied tightly together at the point of the teepee, at the top, with string made from animal guts. Warm furs were laid over this structure and sewn tightly in place. Large rocks were piled around the bottom, to help hold the hut together." [from "All You Need to Know about Neanderthals" by Dr. William Tietjen]

MYTH Velociraptor was a large, intelligent, lizardlike dinosaur.

BULLSHIT! Velociraptor was practically unknown to the public before *Jurassic Park* and has been causing confusion ever since. When most people think of velociraptor, they remember the large, lizardlike, wickedly smart villains from Spielberg's blockbuster. However, those creatures were not based on the real-life velociraptor, but on a larger

MYTH   Neanderthals were hairier than modern man.

BULLSHIT!   Computer models have shown that excess hair on Neanderthals would have caused overproduction of sweat, which would have frozen on the Neanderthals, potentially leading to death.

North American relative called deinonychus. The real velociraptor was a small animal, about the size of a large dog. It also had a more slender body and a longer snout than deinonychus.

MYTH   Black holes are vacuums.

BULLSHIT!   The gravity of a black hole is slightly less than the gravity of the star that caused it. Black holes are not "cosmic vacuum cleaners"; objects can settle into stable orbits around them just as they would around any other mass in space, including stars.

MYTH   DNA (deoxyribonucleic acid) was discovered by James Watson and Francis Crick, winners of the Nobel Prize.

BULLSHIT!   Many people learn the simplified story that Watson and Crick discovered DNA, probably because they won the Nobel Prize for their discovery of its double-helix. The true discoverer was Friedrich Miescher, who was analyzing pus cell nuclei in 1868 when he discovered nuclein. He was able to analyze this further and discovered an acid component, which he called deoxyribonucleic acid. Scientists Oswald Avery, Colin MacLeod, and Maclyn McCarty were the first to show a link between DNA and heredity in 1943, and in 1952 Rosalind Franklin did the first X-ray diffraction pattern study of DNA. What Watson and Crick did was develop a model of DNA that accounted for all of the previous research discoveries.

MYTH   Meteorites are red-hot.

BULLSHIT!   We've all seen the cartoons where a meteor falls to earth (at which point it becomes a meteorite) with a red-hot tinge and smoke blowing off it in all directions. In truth, small meteorites are cold when they hit earth—in fact, many are found with frost on them. A meteorite has been in the near-absolute zero temperature of space for billions of years, so the interior of it is very cold. A meteor's great speed is enough to melt its outside layer, but any molten material will be quickly blown off, and the interior of the meteor does not have time to heat up because rocks are poor conductors of heat. Also, atmospheric drag can slow small meteors to terminal velocity by the time they hit the ground, giving them time to cool down.

MYTH   Dinosaurs were slow and clumsy.

BULLSHIT!   There is no evidence of this. They were (in all likelihood) as mobile as large modern animals—think lions.

MYTH   Tyrannosaurus rex was a lizardlike monster with a square, plain-looking skull, a long tail being dragged on the ground, and a tripodlike stance.

BULLSHIT!   Up to 14 yards long and weighing up to 7 tons, tyrannosaurus rex, the bone-crushing predator, has a long history of inaccurate portrayals. In real life, tyrannosaurus walked in a horizontal stance, with the tail held above the ground. Although this means it was actually shorter than the classic, tripod-rex version, it also means that it was a much more agile animal, able to run at high speed and quickly capture prey with its massive jaws. Its head was not square, and it was not as lizardlike as old movies had made us believe. It actually had a unique shape, different from any other dinosaur, with a narrow snout, eyes that looked forward (giving it highly accurate depth perception), and a series of knobs over the snout which were probably covered with keratin when the animal was alive.

MYTH   *Venusian* is the term to describe Venus and Venus-related things.

BULLSHIT! The correct term is *Cytherean*, which comes from Cytheria–the small island where Aphrodite emerged from a shell. Furthermore, Venusian is also not correct in that it doesn't follow the pattern used for other planets; if you aren't referring to Venus as the Cytherian planet, you should call it the Venerean planet.

MYTH   Shaving hair makes it grow back thicker or coarser.

BULLSHIT!   The reason that so many people believe this is that uncut hair ends up developing a taper—or split ends—which feels softer than freshly cut hair. It is for this reason that a man's beard feels soft, but stubble feels rough. Of course, if this myth were true, every balding man would simply get a haircut in order to make his hair grow back thicker. This is also true for women with thinning hair.

MYTH   If you cut a worm in two, it will continue to live as two worms.

BULLSHIT!   A worm can in fact survive being cut in half, but only one half can survive the operation; the other half dies.

MYTH   Penis-enlargement devices work.

BULLSHIT!   Sadly, this is the source of millions of spam emails sent all over the world every day. Vacuum pumps, pills, stretching techniques: None of them make one iota of difference to the size of your manhood (and consequently the engine size of your car). The only way to enlarge your penis is to have enhancement surgery. This is, obviously, extremely expensive, extremely painful, and extremely gruesome— or so I am told!

MYTH   Plants convert carbon dioxide into the oxygen we breathe.

BULLSHIT!   Where do we get the oxygen we breathe? Most people will say it is from plants, which convert the carbon dioxide we emit into oxygen. I suspect this will come as a surprise to most people, but although plants do produce oxygen, they do not do it by converting carbon dioxide. The process by which this all happens is called photosynthesis, and it's relatively complex. To put it simply, plants convert carbon dioxide into carbohydrate precursors and water (fuel for the plant). This is a light, independent process—the plant doesn't need light to perform this task. So how do plants make oxygen for us to breathe? They take light and convert it to potential energy. The by-product of this process is oxygen.

MYTH   Bats are blind.

BULLSHIT!   Bats actually have fairly normal eyesight, although they are very photosensitive and often dazzled by excessive light. However, bats do often use echolocation in situations where their eyesight fails them, such as times of darkness.

MYTH   Chameleons change color to match their environment.

BULLSHIT!   An interesting and fun idea, sure, but simply not true. Though chameleons can be perceived to change their color to match their background, a chameleon's color change is actually the expression of the physical and physiological condition of the lizard. Chameleons are already naturally camouflaged to match their surroundings, and they change their colors depending on their mood and sometimes a form of communication. A chameleon that is frightened, for example, will turn black.

MYTH   A duck's quack does not echo.

BULLSHIT!   This rumor somehow worked up a cult following on the Internet. It got to the point where a respected scientist actually decided to take valuable time out of his day, when he could have been curing cancer or something else unimportant, to test this theory. Trevor Cox of the University of Salford, England, confirmed what all of us logical people knew all along—a duck's quack does echo. He placed a duck in a reverberation chamber and tested its quack. Sure enough he concluded that a duck's quack does echo, though the sound that comes back is very soft due to the fading nature of the actual quack. Hooray for science.

MYTH   The elephant is the only mammal that can't jump.

BULLSHIT!   First of all, just so you know, it is true that adult elephants can't jump—if by jumping we mean the state of having no feet on the ground at the

MYTH Lemmings throw themselves off cliffs, committing suicide in a bizarre natural method of keeping the populace under control.

BULLSHIT! This is entirely untrue. The myth came about because of the Disney film *White Wilderness*, in which lemmings were filmed throwing themselves off cliffs. What really happened is the film crew used brooms to push the lemmings off the cliff.

same time after propelling oneself from a stationary position. But contrary to the popular myth, there are other animals who can't jump. First, the sloth is unable to jump, which suits its lazy lifestyle rather well. Rhinoceroses and hippopotamuses cannot jump either, though unlike elephants, when they run it is possible for them to have all four feet off the ground.

MYTH   One dog year equals seven years to a human.

BULLSHIT!   Dog years are one great big myth. The bogus fact that one dog year is equal to seven human years is usually worked out so that a dog life is equal to a human life in total years, but the numbers just don't add up. The average human life expectancy is 78, while the average dog life expectancy (in false dog years) would equal around 90 years. Furthermore, different dog breeds have dramatically different life expectancies, ranging from a short 6 years to 13 or more years (in general, the smaller the dog, the longer its life expectancy). Furthermore, dogs have a very short "childhood" and a very long middle age, making the comparison completely invalid.

MYTH   Polar bears are left-handed.

BULLSHIT!   The source of this strange idea is now lost in the dark recesses of history, but it is extraordinarily widespread, with more Google results announcing it as gospel than not. But in reality, scientists who have spent their working lives studying polar bears have found that they are actually ambidextrous (they use both "hands" equally well). It is possible that the myth was started when it was observed that the bears work well with their left hands, but people neglected to notice that they also worked well with their right.

MYTH   Traditionally, Saint Bernard dogs were used to help revive people lost in the snowy mountains by carrying a cask of brandy around their necks.

BULLSHIT!   I am sure everyone is familiar with this image. What most people don't know is the fact that it is entirely made up. Saint Bernard dogs have never been used to carry small barrels of brandy. In

fact, alcohol can make hypothermia worse, so the whole idea is not only fake, it is dangerous. The famous monks at the travelers hospice in the Saint Bernard Pass (where the name of the dogs originated) state that they have never put brandy casks on their rescue dogs, but they do keep a few flasks lying around for the tourists' photos.

MYTH Cracking your knuckles will cause arthritis in later life.

BULLSHIT! The cracking sound in the knuckles is caused by the bones moving apart and forming a gas bubble; the sound is the bubble bursting. It is quite common to hear someone warning a knuckle-cracker that he will get arthritis, but the worst that can happen to a compulsive-cracker is that their finger joints may weaken over time. Arthritis is caused by a variety of factors, such as crystal formations in the case of gout, but knuckle cracking isn't one of them.

MYTH Goldfish are often thought of as having very short memories, usually up to a few seconds at the most.

BULLSHIT! In fact, goldfish have been trained to navigate mazes, and after a few months, a goldfish can recognize its owner.

MYTH In ten years there will be no bananas left.

BULLSHIT! There is some basis in truth to this myth (as is often the case)—there is a disease called fusarium wilt, or Panama disease, that is threatening bananas in some Asian countries, and the variety at risk is the banana most Americans are familiar with, the Cavendish banana. But the disease is not likely to wipe out the entire world's stock of bananas—or even the Cavendish banana—as some of the larger exporting farms are not infected. Furthermore, the Cavendish is only one of roughly 300 types of bananas that are available and suitable for human consumption. Interesting fact: Bananas don't grow on trees—the plant that produces the banana is actually an herb.

MYTH Hair and fingernails continue to grow after a person dies.

BULLSHIT! The most likely cause of this myth is shrinkage of the skin after death, which gives the false appearance of nail growth.

MYTH   Opening windows will spare your house, or any other building, from a tornado's destructive power.

BULLSHIT!   The strongest tornado on record measured 318 miles per hour, which is more than sufficient to blast any building into pieces, except for structures made of steel-reinforced concrete, and even then, the building must be short or the wind will blow it over.

MYTH   The older you get the grumpier you get.

BULLSHIT!   A recent study found that our personalities don't change much after age 30. So, if you're cheerful and gregarious in your forties, you can expect to be the same in your eighties. Marked personality changes some seniors experience are due not to normal aging but to some related disease like dementia or stroke. This is something worth considering when you are planning to marry in your thirties—your future spouse probably behaves now the same way he or she will for the rest of his or her life.

MYTH   All black bears are black.

BULLSHIT!   They also come in white, brown, cinnamon, and blue, depending on where in the world they are found.

MYTH   The white rhinoceros is named that way because of its color.

BULLSHIT!   The white rhinoceros is so-called not because it is white (it is actually gray-brown); in this context, "white" is a corruption of the Afrikaans word *wijd*, which means "wide" and refers to the animal's lips.

MYTH   Pandas only eat bamboo.

BULLSHIT!   Pandas love bamboo, but it isn't their only source of food. The reason that pandas eat so much bamboo is that it doesn't run away. They are omnivores that have adapted to a primarily bamboo diet, but they will eat anything they can catch, including small animals and carrion. The problem is that bamboo doesn't provide a lot of energy, so pandas can become too slow to catch anything else—a vicious cycle. There are a couple of great articles by *National Geographic* from the 1980s about the pandas.

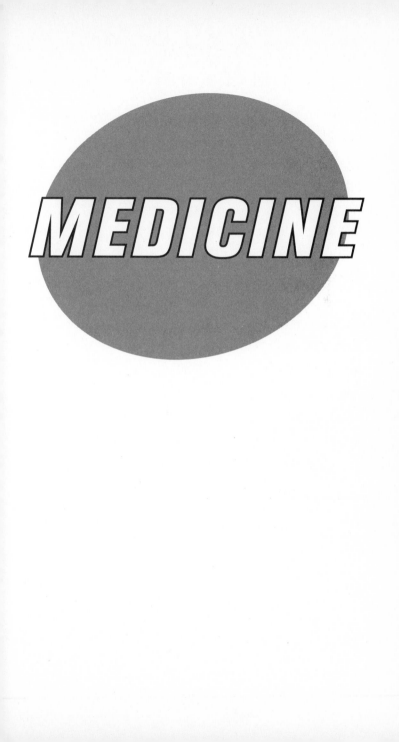

MYTH Sugar makes kids hyperactive.

BULLSHIT! Dr. Rachel C. Vreeman and Dr. Aaron E. Carroll, both pediatricians at the Riley Hospital for Children in Indianapolis, recently said, "In at least 12 double-blinded, randomized, controlled trials, scientists have examined how children react to diets containing different levels of sugar. None of these studies, not even studies looking specifically at children with attention

deficit hyperactivity disorder, could detect any differences in behavior between the children who had sugar and those who did not." This includes artificial and natural sources of sugar. Interestingly, in the study, parents who were told their children had been given sugar when they hadn't noted that the child was more hyperactive. So it seems it is all in the parent's mind.

MYTH Somebody who avoids social interaction is "antisocial."

BULLSHIT! This is mostly a semantic error. Many people refer to someone who is reluctant to participate in social situations as antisocial. In fact, these people are often pro-social, even unusually so. Antisocial Personality Disorder is diagnosed in adults who consistently ignore the rights of others by behaving violently, lying, stealing, or generally acting recklessly with no concern for the safety of themselves or others. They are often extroverted and very much the opposite of the type of people who are so often called antisocial, who usually care very much about other people's feelings.

MYTH All cancers are the same.

BULLSHIT! Slogans promoting a "cure for cancer" make people assume there is essentially one drug that will fix one illness. There are more than 100 types of cancer, and they are all approached differently, depending on how much is known about the specific cancer and on the patient's specific needs. Thanks to the fund-raising efforts

MYTH   You can catch the flu from a flu shot.

BULLSHIT!   Well—rumors be damned—you can't. Flu shots are made of viruses that have been deactivated or killed. Despite the virus not being alive, your body is still able to recognize it for what it is and will try to do something about it, but you do not actually have the flu. Having said that, there was a case of enormous quantities of swine flu vaccine being recalled because the lab forgot to deactivate the virus. Oops.

of organizations such as Susan G. Komen and Avon, medicine has made great advances in breast cancer research. Other diseases, like pancreatic and esophageal cancers, are relatively out of the spotlight and as such, much is still being discovered and survival rates are still comparatively low.

MYTH Surgery could cause cancer to spread throughout the body.

BULLSHIT! This myth probably originated decades before, when physicians could only diagnose the most advanced stages of cancer and surgeries were exploratory. Cancer treatment was still pretty rudimentary, and without modern machinery, there was no way to fully determine if every cancerous cell was removed. Equipment has vastly improved since then and can provide a much clearer picture of what needs to be done during surgery.

MYTH Your heart stops when you sneeze.

BULLSHIT! This is a myth that at least has some basis in real observations. The belief that the heart stops when you sneeze is false, but the reason that this myth has come about is that, in some cases, a sneeze can cause a slightly erratic heartbeat. This is merely due to a change in pressure inside the chest.

MYTH   The older you are, the less sleep you need.

BULLSHIT!   In fact, the rate of sleep needed is fairly constant throughout our adult life, but once we get over the age of 65, we need a little extra sleep. The most likely reason for this myth is that old people can have more difficulty getting to sleep, and this reduces the overall quantity taken. But it is inability to sleep that is the problem here—not a lack of need.

MYTH   You lose most of your body heat through your head.

BULLSHIT!   A military study many years ago tested the loss of warmth in soldiers when exposed to very cold temperatures. They found rapid heat loss in the head—and so the idea that we lose heat through our heads was born. But what they didn't tell you was that the soldiers were fully clothed except for their heads. This obviously skews the statistics considerably. The fact is, completely naked, you lose approximately 10 percent of your body heat through the head—the other 90 percent is lost via the other parts of your body.

MYTH   People with Dissociative Identity Disorder
(DID) radically change their behavior and lose their
memory of what has just been happening when they
switch personalities.

BULLSHIT!   People with DID have anywhere
from two to more than 100 different personalities
that alternately take over their bodies. These alternate
personalities ("alters") usually, but not always, form
due to childhood trauma. The alters don't always
cause huge, noticeable changes in appearance or
behavior, so observers might not even notice their
existence. Many people with DID ("multiples") realize
that various alters are present and know who those
people are, even before therapy, which wouldn't
make sense if they had no memory of switching. It's
possible that one personality has no knowledge of
what happened while one of their alters was in charge,
causing a sense of amnesia, but they might be entirely
aware of what is happening and just not actively
involved. The group of alters can usually communicate
to some degree, and might even work together to
hide the fact that they are multiple. Some multiples
prefer not to undergo therapy that would help them to

choose one personality and stop switching because they are perfectly fine living as a team.

MYTH You should drink at least eight glasses of water a day.

BULLSHIT! This myth most likely originates with the fact that in 1945 the U.S. Food and Nutrition Board said that the human body needed around eight glasses of fluid a day. This included the fluid from all of the foods we eat, as well as from drinks like tea and coffee. Somehow over time,

"fluid" turned to "water" and the modern water myth arose. This also lead to silly slogans like, "If you are thirsty it is too late"—a concept that would seem to have been invented by water bottlers with something to gain from people's excess water consumption. If you're thirsty, drink some water. If you're not, don't.

MYTH   A weakened immune system heightens the risks of catching a cold.

BULLSHIT!   In scientific studies, healthy and unhealthy people exhibit the same amount of susceptibility to colds. Interestingly, studies have also found that 95 percent of people who had the cold virus directly applied to their nasal membranes became infected, but only 75 percent of them exhibited any symptoms of the cold. This is called an "asymptomatic infection."

MYTH   Someone who gets amnesia forgets his past and identity.

BULLSHIT!   Amnesia is, basically, memory loss. In books and movies, amnesia usually involves a loss of most or all memories from before the time that the amnesia began. This is not, however, how amnesia usually works. Amnesia is usually caused by some kind of damage to the brain by injury, drugs, or illness, and a type of amnesia called "dissociative amnesia" is created by psychological reasons, usually resulting from a traumatic event. There are two general kinds of amnesia according to their effect: anterograde and retrograde. Anterograde amnesia causes people to have trouble forming new memories. Retrograde amnesia causes people to forget memories that they already had. A lot of people with amnesia suffer from both kinds. For instance, one of the more common kinds of amnesia occurs when someone gets a head injury and forgets both the events leading up to the injury and what happened immediately afterward. A severe form of mixed amnesia could include forgetting some past events as well as having permanent problems with new memories.

MYTH   Most dyslexics don't learn to read.

BULLSHIT!   Dyslexics, if they don't get appropriate help, often learn slowly and stay well below their grade level in reading speed and comprehension. But even that's not always true: Many dyslexic children figure out how to cover up their difficulty reading until third or fourth grade or even longer. And if they

MYTH Mouth ulcers are as contagious as cold sores.

BULLSHIT! If you have ever had a cold sore you know how agonizing they can be. And they are extremely contagious, so no kissing! But unlike cold sores, mouth ulcers are not contagious though many people wrongly think they are. So far, the cause of mouth ulcers is not entirely certain—but viruses and bacteria have been ruled out. They are most likely caused by disturbances in the immune system.

are taught by someone who understands dyslexia, they can learn to read perfectly well.

MYTH Psychopaths are all murderers or serial killers.

BULLSHIT! Psychopaths are self-centered, superficially charming, callous, reckless, fearless and irresponsible, have no empathy for other people or sense of guilt, and often can lie as easily as tell the truth because they don't particularly care whether what they say is true. Certainly, the charm and lack of empathy or guilt would make a psychopath an excellent serial killer. On the other hand, their lack of planning might cause problems when it comes to covering up that crime. Still, even if it would be easy for somebody like this to commit murder, psychopaths may live their lives simply lying and making reckless decisions, not killing people. Plus, many serial killers are psychotic ("crazy" or delusional) or have one of a variety of other problems rather than being psychopathic, so "psychopath" is not a synonym for someone who doesn't mind committing murder.

MYTH   It's good to suck on your finger after you've cut it.

BULLSHIT!   I bet all of you have, at least once, cut your finger and stuck it straight in your mouth. This is bad, bad, bad. The mouth is full of bacteria—it is not a clean environment at all. Sticking your finger in your mouth after cutting it is an open invitation to infection. Where this weird behavior came from I do not know, but let us hope that we all remember this next time we get a cut.

MYTH The prevalence of cancer is on the rise.

BULLSHIT! Contrary to what many of us believe, it's not so. It's true that there are more cases of cancer than in the past, but this doesn't take into account many other factors, such as increased population and longevity (risk for certain cancers increases with age). When compared to populations of the past, there is actually a decrease in the risk of cancer. This misconception may be prevalent simply because the topic is no longer taboo and people hear about it more often than they did in the past.

MYTH You should never swallow gum.

BULLSHIT! I am sure we have all been told at least once by a concerned adult not to swallow gum, as it will take seven years to leave our bodies. This is right up there with the whole "fruit seed growing a tree in your stomach" silliness, but while most adults realize the tree story is a myth, they don't see that the gum one is too. It is true that gum is not digestible in the

MYTH Schizophrenic people hear voices in their heads.

BULLSHIT! We've all heard about schizophrenia, and we've all heard jokes about "the voices in my head." But, contrary to what a lot of people believe, not all people with schizophrenia hear voices in their heads. Auditory hallucinations are very common in schizophrenic people, but they are more likely to hear voices coming from some object outside of their body than inside their mind.

human body, but it simply passes whole through your system. It doesn't stick to your insides; it just continues along with any food you have eaten and pops out the other end. This myth may have partly arisen from the fact that swallowing gum was once viewed as lower class and ignorant.

MYTH   The symptoms of a cold (running nose, coughing, etc.) are designed to help us get over the sickness quickly.

BULLSHIT!   Many people believe this to be true and therefore they don't think that we should treat

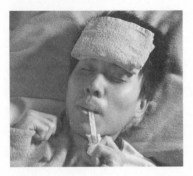

the symptoms with medicines. But the truth is that the symptoms not only make no difference to the duration of the cold, they can help spread the bug to other people—through nose blowing and coughing. You should take comfort in knowing that painkillers and other cold medicines will not only make the illness more tolerable, they will help to keep it contained.

MYTH   Depression only affects a person's mood.

BULLSHIT!   Depression is, by far, the most common mental illness in the United States, with about 17 percent of people suffering from clinical depression at some point in their life. Depression causes persistent, long-term feelings of sadness and hopelessness, and a lack of interest in activities that the depressed person once enjoyed. It's easy to think that depression is only an emotional problem, but depression also has a lot of relations to the physical body as well. First, depression can be caused by physical reasons, most commonly as an imbalance of chemicals in the body. Chronic pain and some physical illnesses also cause depression. At the same time, people often feel more pain when they are depressed, either because they are more stressed, they are dwelling on their pain more, or depression just causes pain to become worse. Depression also usually causes people to sleep more or less and eat more or less, depending on the individual, and those habits have a major physical effect. There are various other connections between depression and the physical body as well.

MYTH   Teething causes a fever in babies.

BULLSHIT!   Scientific studies have been done that show no correlation at all between fever and teething. If your baby is suffering from a new tooth and has a fever, it is advisable to check for other causes of the fever. The same is true of diarrhea, which is also often blamed on teething in infants. It is always better to be safe than sorry when dealing with the health of children.

MYTH   Dyslexics see words backward or out of order.

MYTH   People who intentionally cut, burn, or otherwise injure themselves are trying to kill themselves or looking for attention.

BULLSHIT!   No matter what it looks like, self-injury is not a failed suicide attempt. Some self-injurers harm themselves over and over for years without inflicting a single life-threatening injury. This would be an amazing record of failure if they were actually trying to die. Many people who self-injure are actually trying to avoid suicide by letting out their feelings in a (somewhat) safer way.

BULLSHIT!   This can seem to be the case because, in their confusion while they try to figure out a word, they mix up letters or sounds, and some dyslexic people confuse left and right or have a lot of trouble spelling. However, this is not the cause of their problem. Dyslexia has much more to do with a unique way of thinking than a problem with processing visual information.

MYTH   Cancer treatment is painful and pointless— and cancer isn't curable.

BULLSHIT!   Although this may have been almost true 30 years ago, medical advances have brought modern cancer treatments that are far more effective and cause less suffering for the patient. A few decades ago, 90 percent of children with leukemia died; today 80 percent survive. Many people think cancer is incurable because there isn't a "one drug fixes all" cure, but many people are completely cured of cancer. Various drugs exist to treat different types of cancer, and many of them are extremely effective and well worth trying if you do get the disease.

MYTH   You can sweat a cold out.

BULLSHIT!   We have all done it—or at least seen others do it: covering up with extra blankets, sticking your head over a bowl of hot water, all in the hopes that we will sweat the cold out. Unfortunately, this does not work—it is completely ineffective. The only benefit this may have is to make you feel a little better (because it addresses the symptoms).

MYTH   Medical science already has and is withholding a cure for cancer.

BULLSHIT!   Conspiracy theories abound, and like many, this one is false. Doctors take the Hippocratic oath because they are committed to saving lives, which a cure for cancer would surely do. If that doesn't convince you, then surely you can see that any pharmaceutical company would want to be the first to claim ownership of a cash cow like the cure for cancer. Recently a drug was tested on four dogs that had cancers previously thought to be too advanced to be treated—the drug cured them. With a few more successful cases, researchers will soon be allowed to see if this drug could yield similar results in humans.

MYTH   Manic episodes in a bipolar sufferer are usually enjoyable times of great creativity.

BULLSHIT!   This is a myth that can sometimes be true. People who suffer from bipolar disorder have alternating periods of depression and an elevated mood known as mania. Mania usually involves feelings of happiness, energy, inappropriately high self-esteem, and lack of inhibition or self-control. This can allow creativity to come more easily, because a manic person will just use their ideas without considering how good or bad they are. Some artists or writers with manic depression actually do not want treatment because their manic episodes are so useful to them, even if the depression is miserable. On the other hand, there are a lot of negative aspects of mania, like a shortened attention span and a lack of sleep. The lack of inhibitions can cause spending sprees that the person cannot afford, inappropriate social behavior, or dangerously reckless actions. Mania can also cause irritability and a short temper, as much as it can create pleasant feelings, and it may impair a person's life as much as depression does.

MYTH   Back pain should be treated with bed rest.

BULLSHIT!   The opposite is actually true in this case. Bed rest can prevent the lower back from fully recovering—or at the very least, delay the recovery significantly. Patients who continue to engage in ordinary activities recover faster and usually have fewer problems with recurring pain and other back troubles. Interestingly, many studies have shown that this is not just true of back problems, but also many other medical problems. Thirty-nine independent studies found bed rest to do more harm than good in a broad range of illnesses.

MYTH   There is no cure for cancer.

BULLSHIT!   It is not true. It gets a bit confusing because we delve into technicalities but while the disease is incurable so far, the individual cancer patient can be cured. So, while it's technically true that cancer isn't curable, it's also horribly wrong and very much false to tell someone they can't be cured of their cancer. As far as individuals are concerned, there is a cure for their cancer. A patient's cancer is considered to be in remission if they are cancer free for some period during the first five years after diagnosis. If after treatment and after those five years there is no recurrence of the cancer, then the patient is declared cured. Certain types, such as skin cancer, are curable by simply removing the tumor. Although childhood leukemia and breast cancer are incurable, 80 to 90 percent of patients undergo successful treatments, become cured, and can live relatively normal lives.

MYTH   Drinking milk while you have a cold is a bad idea because it causes more mucous to build up.

BULLSHIT!   Actually, milk does not cause a buildup of mucous at all—you can drink as much of it as you like, and it will have no effect on your cold.

MYTH   Kissing a person with a cold will cause you to catch it.

BULLSHIT!   The reality is that the quantity of virus on the lips and mouth is minuscule, and a much larger dose would be required for you to become infected. It is the nasal mucous you have to worry about— so no nose-kissing.

MYTH   Autism is a devastating disorder that will stop someone from ever being able to function in society.

BULLSHIT!   Many people hear "autism" and imagine children who are permanently in their own world where they can't talk or interact with anyone else, who throw tantrums for no apparent reason, and who will never be part of normal society. However, autism is called a spectrum disorder for a reason: Autistics range from people who are unable to communicate in any way with others all the way to people who live ordinary, productive lives and just seem a bit eccentric to the rest of us.

MYTH   People with ADHD (Attention Deficit Hyperactivity Disorder) are unable to pay attention to anything.

BULLSHIT!   This is perhaps the most common misconception in psychology. People with ADHD have trouble concentrating on tasks and can be hyperactive or impulsive. But it isn't true, as it sometimes seems, that people with ADHD just can't pay attention. Many of them can pay attention to something that they find genuinely interesting, the same way all of us are much more willing to be distracted from a dull task than from an enjoyable one. And, in fact, some people have trouble focusing because they actually pay too much attention. They think about all the sights, sounds, and smells around them, not just the task at hand. They have to learn to deal with all the other interesting stimuli and keep most of their attention on what is important.

MYTH   Eating at night makes you fat.

BULLSHIT!   Secret snackers rejoice! This is a complete myth. It doesn't matter what time of day you eat; as long as you eat only the total calories that you burn each day, you will not gain weight. If you eat fewer calories than you burn, you will lose weight, and if you eat more calories, you will gain. It is as simple as that. Having said that, the routine of three meals a day at the same time each day can have other benefits in life (routine is good and it helps humans work more effectively), but snacks at night are no worse than snacks in the morning or afternoon.

MYTH   Most people with Tourette's syndrome swear uncontrollably.

BULLSHIT!   People with Tourette's syndrome have two kinds of tics: motor and vocal. The most common motor tic is excessive eye blinking. Other examples are grimacing, or moving arms or legs. The most common vocal tic is actually throat clearing, but vocal tics can also include saying words, making meaningless sounds, or even repeating what someone else has said (echolalia). Tics in themselves aren't usually a problem, but they can be annoying and cause negative reactions from other people (particularly if the vocal tic does involve inappropriate words). TS can be related to ADHD and obsessive-compulsive disorder.

MYTH   Eating turkey makes you sleepy because it contains tryptophan.

BULLSHIT!   This is one of the most common myths on this list, and it pops up every year around Thanksgiving. But actually, chicken and ground beef contain almost identical quantities of tryptophan as turkey does. Other foods such as cheese and pork contain significantly more of the chemical than turkey. So why do people think turkey makes them sleepy? It is most likely due to turkey appearing at very large meals often eaten during the day rather than the evening. The heavy meal slows blood flow, which can cause drowsiness, and the timing can have a huge psychological impact. In other words, you are imagining it.

MYTH   Cell phones cause cancer.

BULLSHIT!   The fact of the matter is that technology is advancing rapidly and cell phones now contain far fewer carcinogens than their predecessors. Studies on the correlation of cell phones to brain cancer are difficult, because it's hard to accurately document such a study. However, the most recent attempt was done by the Danish Cancer Society, and no link between cell phones and brain cancer was found.

MYTH   People with bulimia always purge by inducing vomiting.

BULLSHIT!   Bulimia is one of a large number of eating disorders. People with bulimia are intensely concerned either with losing weight or maintaining their current weight. However, they can't, or don't want to, avoid eating altogether, so they eat a normal or unusually large amount of food (binge) and then find some way to get rid of it (purge). The binge-purge cycles are usually not entirely under the person's conscious control, especially not after the person has been bulimic for a long time. One of the most

MYTH   "Feed a cold, starve a fever."

BULLSHIT!   Eating has no negative impact on the body when you are sick; in fact, the opposite is true. Food provides the body with fuel to cope with illness—so when we are sick, it is a good idea to eat healthy and well. I recommend a good bowl of chicken soup for a start!

common ways to purge is to induce vomiting. There are, however, other ways. Many bulimic people use laxatives, diuretics, or diet pills. Others exercise to work off the weight they believe they gained from a meal, or they fast in compensation for the food they ate when they binged. So, just because somebody does not throw up after meals does not mean that they are not bulimic.

MYTH It is harder to lose weight than to gain weight.

BULLSHIT! Actually, once you get your head around a new eating pattern, math and science are working in your favor. It is mathematically easier to lose than to gain. For example, if you eat 3,500 calories more than you burn, you will gain 0.3 pounds, but if you burn 3,500 calories more than you eat, you will lose 1 pound. Also, if you want to lose weight, you can expose yourself to significant changes in temperature, which speeds up your metabolism. Finally, the above information is based on a pure fat diet—variations to the math occur when you introduce other types of food.

MYTH Some people have a contact lens stuck permanently behind their eye.

BULLSHIT! People who claim to have this condition will usually use a fear of having their eyeball popped out to retrieve it as the main reason they have just left the contact there. Well here is the good news for those of you who think you may be suffering this annoying side-effect to contact lens wearing: It is impossible for a contact lens to get stuck behind your eye. There is no cavity behind the eye for it to go to. So if you think you have lost your lens, the most likely place to find it is either tucked into a ball in your eyelid, or on the bathroom floor where you drunkenly tried to remove it!

MYTH Artificial sweeteners cause cancer.

BULLSHIT! This is a misconception that has regularly shown up in news headlines since the 1970s because of a 1969 study on the effects of cyclamate on mice. It was later disclosed that the mice had been given the cyclamate equivalent of 800 cans of diet soda per day for several weeks. No studies observing moderate amounts of artificial sweeteners have shown a link to cancer. Artificial

sweeteners are discussed here because this is a prevalent food myth, but the principle involved applies to many other kitchen goods, from coffee to broccoli to even water (specifically, the fluoride content in water). Too much of anything could lead to cancer, but it requires an excessive amount of the product to be potentially hazardous.

MYTH   You can lose a tampon inside the vagina.

BULLSHIT!   This is one for the women (and one the men may want to skip). It is surprisingly common for women to visit the emergency room because their tampon string fell off, and they can't find their tampon. In almost every case, the investigating doctor will find nothing inside. The reason for this? There is nowhere for it to go. The walls of the vagina are closed together until something is put between them (in this case a tampon). At the top of the potential space created in the vagina by an object is the cervix. If a tampon is missing, it is probably because you forgot you removed it.

MYTH   Somebody with selective mutism is either refusing to speak, or has been abused or traumatized in the past.

BULLSHIT!   If you don't know someone with selective mutism, chances are you still believe in a myth very common in the media: Some children and teenagers stop talking entirely, or to everyone but one or two people, because they were traumatized or repeatedly abused. While some people do become mute after trauma, this usually lasts a few weeks, not months or years. Most people do not develop selective mutism in later childhood or because of any kind of trauma or abuse. Most selectively mute people do want to talk, but don't because they're actually afraid to. An overwhelming majority of selectively mute people also suffer from social anxiety disorder, and silence seems to be one way that they cope with stressful situations.

MYTH   All lumps or large masses detected during cancer screenings are cancerous.

BULLSHIT!   Not every abnormality is an automatic cancer diagnosis. It could just be a cyst that would either reabsorb itself into the body or need to be surgically removed. Some tumors are benign, meaning they are noncancerous. However, screenings are important to determine which tumors are benign, precancerous, and cancerous.

MYTH   People with obsessive compulsive disorder are always obsessed with the danger of germs, and usually are very particular about neatness.

BULLSHIT!   OCD is an anxiety disorder with two characteristics. First, people with OCD have recurring unwanted thoughts (obsessions), usually of something they find disturbing or not at all in their character. Second, these people think that doing some certain ritual will get rid of the danger. Not everyone who has OCD cares about germs or does the rituals that we usually hear about. Not everyone even has compulsions an observer would actually notice, since a lot of those compulsions are mental.

MYTH   Agoraphobia is a fear of open places.

BULLSHIT!   *Agoraphobia* literally means "fear of the marketplace." It is often considered to be a fear of open or public places. People who suffer from panic attacks often develop agoraphobia because they want to avoid any situation that might cause an attack. Other people with agoraphobia haven't actually had panic attacks, but are afraid of similar things—for instance, a sense that they will pass out. Agoraphobia can be so severe that someone who suffers from it may be unable even to leave the house. But agoraphobia is not specifically a fear of open places. Instead, it is a fear of places that the phobic person cannot easily escape from if they need to for some reason—most likely if they start to have a panic attack. An open area offers few places to hide within a short distance, and a public place would be embarrassing to get out of. I've even heard a suggestion that agoraphobia is most similar to claustrophobia, in that it is a fear of being trapped somewhere.

MYTH Only women get breast cancer.

BULLSHIT! Women are 100 times more likely to get breast cancer than men, but since men also have breast tissue, it is still possible for them to develop breast cancer. The American Cancer

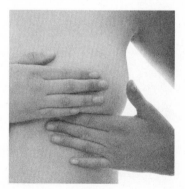

Society states that roughly 2,000 men are diagnosed with breast cancer every year.

MYTH   You can inject a drug directly into a person's heart in order for the drug to work as quickly as possible.

BULLSHIT!   *Pulp Fiction* is a brilliant film, but unfortunately it perpetuates this myth. In the film, a shot of adrenaline is given directly into the heart after a drug overdose. Unfortunately it is entirely mythical. Doctors never, ever inject a person directly into the heart. Adrenaline is delivered in the case of heart attack, but it is delivered directly to a vein. Also, adrenaline is not used to treat heroin overdose—narcan is. The closest that doctors come to putting a needle near your heart is when they insert it into the surrounding sac to remove excess fluids.

MYTH   All you need to beat cancer is a positive attitude, not treatment.

BULLSHIT!   This is a dangerous untruth. A good attitude does wonders to help alleviate the gravity of the situation. That's why so many members of the cancer ward medical staff have a very pleasant demeanor. It certainly helps that the patient can

MYTH   Lots of vitamin C and zinc help to stave off (or cure) a cold.

BULLSHIT!   Though it is often a good idea to take vitamin and mineral supplements, they have no effect on the cold virus. Once the cold hits, you are better off taking painkillers and waiting it out.

maintain a positive outlook throughout treatment. However, cancer is much more than "mind over matter," and thus far, western medical research has provided the only avenue that has been repeatedly and comprehensively studied, and consistently proves to be the most effective treatment against cancer.

MYTH   Mental disorders and illnesses are all in your head, and you can just get over them if you really want to.

BULLSHIT!   Some people still believe that mental illnesses are all imagined, or that people

157

who suffer from mental illness can't really be having that much trouble and/or just don't care enough about getting over it. People are especially likely to be dismissive if the illness isn't well-known, and so many of them, even common ones, are not. The fact that the same symptoms have been experienced by so many different people should prove that mental illnesses are real—these people can't all be independently inventing the same symptoms. Any mental disorder, by definition, seriously affects the lives of the people who suffer from it, usually for the worse, or it would not be considered a disorder. And mental illnesses are certainly not easy to get over. Most mental disorders are caused at least in part by a difference in the brain or an imbalance of chemicals. Even when it comes to the nonphysical reasons, it's very difficult to unlearn a thought pattern or habit. Plus, the disorder itself may stop someone from trying to get help: People with depression might think no therapist will be able to help them, and be too tired to try to find one, anyway. If we could overcome mental illnesses just by wanting to, the world would be full of much happier and more productive people.

MYTH   Kids will get acne from eating too much chocolate or greasy food.

BULLSHIT!   Too many kids are berated every day with this warning because "You will get acne!" In fact, there have been very careful scientific studies that show an extremely low probability of acne being caused by either of these things. One such test fed a control group "chocolate" with no chocolate in it, and the other group got chocolate with ten times the usual amount. No changes occurred in either group. But don't forget: Too much of either will make you fat.

MYTH   Most colds are caught in the winter.

BULLSHIT!   Most colds are caught in the spring and fall seasons. This is because the virus becomes much more active in those seasons and seems to become largely dormant in the winter.

MYTH   Falling asleep after getting a concussion is life-threatening.

BULLSHIT!   Ah—yet again we have the movies to blame for this one. In most cases, getting a concussion is not life-threatening, and you don't need to slap your children repeatedly in the face to keep them awake if they bump their heads (unless they have been naughty). Concussion almost never leads to a coma. But remember—if you or someone you know does receive a severe knock to the head, take them to the doctor so they can be sure that everything is okay.

MYTH   Those with learning disabilities are less intelligent than people who don't have them.

BULLSHIT!   It's a common idea that people with learning disabilities, because they learn slowly in classroom environments that are not suited to them, are less intelligent than their peers. In fact, many people with learning disabilities are highly intelligent, and most are unusually creative. Some of them are most intelligent in an area that, unfortunately, isn't emphasized in school, so they struggle in the classes that schools think are most important. These people simply learn and think in different ways from average people, not necessarily in worse ways.

MYTH Nudist resorts and events are places of sexual activity.

BULLSHIT! This is the most untrue misconception about nudism. In fact, any place where true nudism is practiced, sexual activity, exhibitionism, and voyeurism are strictly prohibited, and such conduct results in the offending participant being expelled from the grounds immediately, never to be allowed to re-enter. Sexual activity is not allowed any more in a nudist resort or event than any typical public setting, and the other members are even encouraged to report such conduct, if they see it, to the organizer or owner of the facility.

MYTH There is no such thing as a real ninja.

BULLSHIT! In fact, ninjas and the arts that they learned date back more than 800 years. The ninja families developed their skills in order to protect themselves against the likes of Samurai warriors. It is this humble beginning that gives *ninjutsu* its very unique style: Escape if you can; if you can't, kill. There was nothing unethical to the ninja—he would throw sand in the enemies' eyes, stab them when they

MYTH Black boxes in planes are black.

BULLSHIT! Actually, they are orange. This is to help investigators locate them by sight, if necessary, after a crash. The name was chosen entirely to be humorous.

were down, anything to protect life and limb. Over time, the ninjas were used as spies, bodyguards, and assassins for hire.

MYTH When someone gets what they deserve they get their "just desserts."

BULLSHIT! Just desserts? Does that even make sense? Well, the correct phrase is actually "just deserts," and don't worry if you didn't know that because you're not alone. The reason for this misunderstanding comes from the rarely used noun form of the verb "to deserve"; something that is deserved is a desert (pronounced "dessert"). It's hard to tell when the original word was altered, but it probably had something to do with witty restaurateurs naming their businesses Just Desserts as a pun; the phrase caught on and original was forgotten.

MYTH Nudism is sexually stimulating.

BULLSHIT! Many people, when they try nudism, find themselves surprised at the lack of sexual arousal they experience. Many men are afraid of trying the lifestyle for fear of being visibly aroused. However, nudist facilities usually make it quite clear to men that this hardly ever happens, and to roll over or take a dip in the pool in the small chance that it does. At nudist resorts and events, participants find so many other activities to do and sights to see that arousal is the last thought to come to mind. Many nudists even forget that they, and the other people, are nude. People in a nudist setting actually find that they are less likely to be aroused there than at a beach or pool where people wear bathing suits, for bathing suits actually draw attention to the body parts they are supposed to hide.

MYTH Elevator cables sometimes snap causing free fall and death.

BULLSHIT! Do you have a fear of being caught in an elevator when the cable snaps, sending you into free fall? Fear no longer. First, elevators usually have a minimum of four operating cables, as well as a built-in braking system and a backup braking system in the shaft that forces a wedge into the shaft to prevent too rapid a drop. If the cables were all to snap (and believe me, elevator cables are strong), the car's braking system would detect the free fall and automatically activates. If that, too, were to fail, the

shaft's braking system would take over. There has been one recorded account of a complete elevator free fall; it was caused by an airplane that crashed into the Empire State Building in 1945. The crash caused the cables in the elevator to be weakened, ultimately. causing them to break. The person riding the elevator, Betty Lou Oliver, survived the 75-floor free fall because of air pressure beneath the car.

MYTH Ninjas catch swords with their bare hands.

BULLSHIT! In fact, ninjas are taught that the best way to deal with an incoming sword is to "just get out of the way." Of course, in movies it looks flashy to have a ninja catch a sword, but there would be very little need to do so when a ninja has so many other techniques in his arsenal. Having said that, using claws or other hand weapons, if it were necessary, a ninja might stop a sword with the weapons he is holding—but not with his bare hands.

MYTH All nudists have attractive bodies.

BULLSHIT! Nudists have all kinds of bodies— any kind, size, or shape of body you see in day-to-day life. Many people worry about trying nudism because they are worried they are too fat, have a scar, or just don't look like a supermodel. Anyone is allowed in, and no one ever makes fun of anyone or comments about anyone's body. Nudism is not a beauty contest.

MYTH   You can't fold a piece of paper in half more than seven times.

BULLSHIT!   This is one we all hear regularly, and we believe it because it seemed to be true when we tried it. But in 2002 a high school student named Britney Gallivan proved it wrong by folding a piece of thin gold leaf more than seven times with the use of tweezers. To further prove that it could be done, she bought a giant roll of toilet paper on the Internet and she and her family took it to the local mall, where they attempted to fold it more than seven times. Seven hours later, they had folded it 12 times.

MYTH   Nudism is just for adults.

BULLSHIT!   Nudism welcomes children and actually encourages families with young children to bring their kids. Children are the most enthusiastic nudists because they have not yet learned to feel shame about their own or others' bodies, or to equate nudity with sex. Most venues even have play areas

MYTH Because of double jeopardy, you can't be tried twice for the same crime.

BULLSHIT! In the U.S., a person can be tried twice for the same crime if the crime violates both federal and state law. In these cases, the 5th Amendment is overridden by a 1922 U.S. Supreme Court decision.

and activities set up for children. However, children are only allowed to enter if they are accompanied by their parents or legal guardians, and their parents, organizers, and the other nudists are always on the lookout for anyone who would take advantage of children.

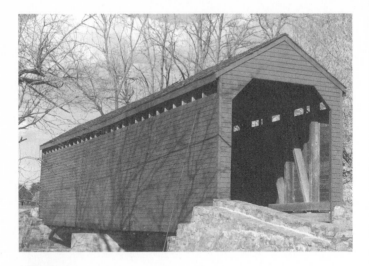

MYTH Covered bridges were usually built to protect people traveling on them.

BULLSHIT! They were built to protect the bridges themselves. This is because early bridges were usually made from wood and needed to be protected from the elements. Keeping the rain off people crossing is just a bonus.

MYTH Shop owners must honor incorrectly advertised prices.

BULLSHIT! Shop owners are frequently hounded by customers who demand a discount, stating that if someone mistakenly advertises a product for the wrong price, they have to sell it at that price. But the reality is a little more bland. A shop price is an "invitation to bargain" not an "invitation to buy." This is true in the United States, United Kingdom, commonwealth nations, and probably the rest of the western world. If a shop makes a mistake, they can simply continue to sell the goods at the normal price. Attempts to defraud by advertising lower prices are addressed in other consumer laws. However, it should be noted that if an electronic transaction is completed, you may be allowed to keep the goods if a mistake is made.

MYTH   Ninjas wore masks and black clothes when fighting.

BULLSHIT!   This is entirely false. These days, most ninjas who are working as bodyguards would wear a suit or similar modern clothing. So when might a ninja have worn a mask? Maybe 800 years ago if they had to hide in the trees, but even then it was not part of a uniform. A ninja wearing a mask and/or black clothing is no different from a soldier wearing camouflage paint. It depends entirely on the environment and the need for hiding.

MYTH   No two countries with McDonald's franchises have ever gone to war.

BULLSHIT!   This theory was proposed by Thomas Friedman and became massively popular all around the world. It was used to show that countries loving democracy (those most likely to have a McDonald's franchise) have lived peacefully together due to the merits of that political system. This is also called the Democratic Peace Theory or the Golden Arches Theory of Conflict Resolution. Friedman's theory is part of his book *The Lexus and the Olive Tree*. But it is not true. Georgia and Russia were recently at war with each other and both have McDonald's. Furthermore, Israel and Lebanon also defy the theory—their conflict took place in 2006—and right after Friedman's book was published, NATO bombed Serbia—again disproving the idea.

MYTH   Nudists remain unclothed all the time.

BULLSHIT!   Nudists remain unclothed any time when practical, but they tend to dress when the weather becomes too cool or rainy, or if they are operating a barbecue or stove. Nudist children who

MYTH James McNeill Whistler's most famous painting is called *Whistler's Mother*.

BULLSHIT! The famous painting *Whistler's Mother* is not actually called that. It was originally called *Arrangement in Grey and Black, No. 1: Portrait of the Painter's Mother*. Whistler later changed it to *Portrait of My Mother*.

are not toilet trained are required to wear swim shorts or a diaper in the pool. Likewise, in the winter, nudist resorts generally close, and the resort owner arranges for events in an indoor setting, such as a swimming pool, gymnasium, or sports facility. Nonetheless, anyone visiting a nudist venue is strongly encouraged to disrobe immediately, or soon after arriving, as a deterrent against voyeurs.

MYTH   The number of hooves in the air on a statue of a horse tells us the fate of its rider.

BULLSHIT!   The idea is that when a statue of a horse has one foot in the air, his rider was wounded in battle but survived. If he has two hooves in the air, the rider was killed, and if he has none in the air, the rider survived. While this is a myth, interestingly it does seem to apply to the majority of statues relating to Gettysburg equestrians—though not to James Longstreet, who was not wounded but his statue does have one leg raised. Interesting fact: A statue of a horse with a rider is called an "equestrian statue"—

which is derived from the Latin *eques* for "knight" and *equus* for "horse." A statue of a horse is called an "equine statue."

MYTH   Ninjas can't kill by just touching a person.

BULLSHIT!   Ninjas can kill just by touch. I bet you weren't expecting that! In fact, there are a series of touches (this word is used lightly, as a decent amount of pressure is needed) that can render a person dead. This is quite logical when you consider that a firm enough blow to the temple can kill a person. The deadly methods are normally only taught to the most advanced students who, by that time, would never need to use them. Fundamental pressure point techniques, however, are taught from the very beginning, and even the most basic student can take a person to the floor with one finger (pressed firmly in the right part of the throat or in the eyeballs, for example). Pressure points cause a lot of pain when pressed in the right way—this is an indispensable tool for the ninja. Furthermore, simple tools like squeezing nipples can also render an offender defenseless in seconds.

MYTH   Nudists are perverts, weirdos, or other sorts of sexually deviant people.

BULLSHIT!   In general, nudists are open, understanding, and extremely friendly. The fact is, you probably don't remember it, but there were days when you could scamper around the house in your birthday suit. Adult nudists tend to be open-minded and willing to listen to others' thoughts, views, and opinions. They are friendly to newcomers and are typically repulsed at even the thought of pornography or sexual immorality.

MYTH   Nudists are asexual people.

BULLSHIT!   Some people think that by treating nudity as not so much a sexual thing, nudists deny human sexuality altogether. In fact, nudists do marry and reproduce, just like nature intended. They just don't include their sexual activities in their lifestyle, as it wouldn't be conducive to an innocent, family atmosphere, and would perpetuate the common misconception that all nudity is sexual. Nudists are sexual beings, but they conduct their activities in private, in their bedrooms, between married partners only.

MYTH   Most Americans opposed the Vietnam War.

BULLSHIT!   Even though there was much vocal opposition to the Vietnam War in the 1960s, research done at the time discovered that 51 percent of young people supported the war. However, 53 percent of those over the age of 30 thought the war was a mistake.

MYTH   Rice paper is made from rice.

BULLSHIT!   It is actually made from the pith of the plant *Tetrapanax papyriferus* (rice paper plant).

MYTH   *Shuriken* (throwing stars) are used to kill at a distance.

BULLSHIT!   *Shuriken* are used as secondary weapons—either to slash or stab. When they are thrown, it is normally to cause a distraction. *Shuriken* come in two varieties: *hira-shuriken* (the famous ninja stars), which were originally household items such as washers and coins that were used to distract and were not usually sharp, and *bo-shuriken*, which are straight spikes up to about 8 inches in length. These were also originally household items, such as chopsticks or hairpins. Their origins certainly make it clear that these were not intended as killing weapons.

MYTH   The United States is the only country that measures things by feet, gallons, pounds, and degrees Fahrenheit.

BULLSHIT!   To demonstrate how out-of-date the U.S. is compared to basically everyone else in the world, it is often pointed out by scientists and metricians that the U.S. still uses the archaic English system. This may be true, but we are not the only ones. Liberia uses the same system, which is not a surprise considering that the country was started by former American slaves who named their capital after American president James Monroe; it was only recently that Liberians elected a president who was not a descendent of the original American emigrants.

And there is a third country that uses the system—
Myanmar. As a former British colony, Myanmar, of
course, adopted the English system. After gaining
independence, the country changed its name (from
Burma), but not how it measured things.

MYTH   Ship captains can legally marry couples
on board.

BULLSHIT!   U.S.
ship captains may not
perform weddings
on board unless the
captain is also a priest,
rabbi, minister, or
other ordained official.
There are even some
regulations specifically
prohibiting shipboard
weddings, even for those
who are competent to
perform the ceremony.

MYTH　Ninjas exclusively use ancient Japanese weapons.

BULLSHIT!　Ninjas are often trained in modern weaponry as well, and many of the so-called ancient weapons are not ancient at all—they are modern takes on ancient concepts (such as the *shuriken*, whose origins lie in coins).

MYTH　Nudists have no sense of privacy.

BULLSHIT!　Although nudists feel comfortable in the nude, they tend to be particularly shy of cameras and have aspects of their life they do not need the world to know. Just because someone is nude, one should not take that as a signal to treat the nudist's life like an open diary, or take pictures as they please. In most nudist settings, photography is restricted or even prohibited, and taking pictures of children (even innocent ones) is strictly forbidden, in order to deter voyeurs and molesters. Likewise, when a person becomes a nudist, the club keeps their information private, just like a person's information is held confidential in any typical public place.

MYTH   Ninjas were able to vanish.

BULLSHIT!   This myth has come about because of the first ninja rule: get away. If a ninja can avoid fighting, he will. In order to achieve this goal, he might need to create a diversion of some kind, such as throwing *shuriken*, setting off a smoke bomb, or throwing sand in the opponent's eyes. By the time the opponent recovered from the distraction, the ninja would be gone. There is no magic involved here—just common sense.

MYTH   Nudism is illegal.

BULLSHIT!   Some people think that nudist venues are a branch of some kind of black market, and that nudists keep their lifestyles secret and unknown to law enforcement for fear of being arrested and prosecuted. While I cannot speak for every jurisdiction on the planet, in most places, laws do not strictly target nudism. In most countries, it is simply illegal to be nude in a public place, and law enforcement generally treats nudist venues as being exempt from that law as everyone who visits agrees to be nude, and the venue is kept out of public view. Many nudists advertise and communicate their lifestyle through the media, and law enforcement treats their lifestyle as a legitimate cause. Some nudists are even police officers, judges, or lawyers themselves. However, there are a few jurisdictions where this misconception is a reality. Nudism is officially illegal in the state of Arkansas, and in the countries of Iran, Iraq, and Saudi Arabia. Sometimes, the police even make frivolous arrests, such as a crackdown on a nude beach, or arresting typical parents who take innocent nude photos of their young children, but in these cases, the court usually sees reason and dismisses the charges as unlawful and unsubstantiated.

MYTH   Ninjas need to be strong and fast.

BULLSHIT!   In fact, the whole point of *ninjutsu* is to use your body effectively—whether you are fat or thin, short or tall. You don't need speed; in fact,

MYTH *Ninjutsu* refers to fighting methods.

BULLSHIT! Actually, it means the art of stealth and perseverance; it is about the strategy and tactics of fighting. The actual moves are from a variety of different martial art disciplines. In the most common and most authentic version of *ninjutsu (Bujinkan Budō Taijutsu)*, 18 disciplines form the main basis of training.

speed can work against you. What you need is the ability to predict your opponent's move and outthink him. Through calm and steady movements you gain control of the enemy and, ultimately, the fight. Much of *ninjutsu* is about foot movement and natural positioning. This allows the ninja to retain his balance in all manner of unusual situations.

MYTH   Nudism is new and alien to the history of humankind.

BULLSHIT!   Humans began naked, both historically and biblically. Many believe that humans originally began to wear clothes as a means to keep warm. Then, over many millennia, clothes evolved to denote status and class. Clothes also slowly evolved to the point where a body without clothes was taboo. However, if you visit the ancient cathedrals in England, you will see many innocent statues of undressed humans, and many great artists, such as Renoir, Donatello, and Michelangelo depicted nude subjects. Nudist clubs and resorts are relatively new in North America—the movement is about a century old—but the swimsuit is also a new invention, prior to which people swam and used saunas in the nude. When the swimsuit was created, it covered most of the body but has been gradually covering less of the body with time. If you put on your swimsuit today and went back in time 100 years to a beach, you would probably get arrested, but go back 200 years and people will wonder why you're dressed at all.

MYTH   In 1839, Abner Doubleday invented baseball.

BULLSHIT!   Actually he didn't. This misconception was derived from a dubious testimony to a committee set up in 1905 to uncover the sport's origins. One man said, "The first scheme for playing baseball, according to the best evidence obtainable to date, was devised by Abner Doubleday at Cooperstown, New York, in 1839." In reality, no one really knows where or when the game was invented, but the first written rules were penned by Alexander Joy Cartwright (1820–1892), and Congress has officially credited him as a the inventor.

MYTH   Lizzie Borden took an axe…

BULLSHIT!   We all know the poem, now you can know the truth. She didn't take an axe, she didn't give anyone 40 whacks (in fact, her father was axed 11 times and her stepmother 18 or 19 times). Lizzie was put on trial for the crime but was found innocent due to the fact that her clothing had no blood on it minutes after the crime. Also adding weight to her defense is the little-known fact that just shortly before her trial, another axe murder happened in the area.

MYTH   President Washington owned a set of wooden teeth.

BULLSHIT!   He did, however, own a set of hippopotamus ivory teeth, as well as horse teeth,

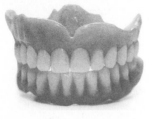

donkey teeth, and human teeth (from various sources), a set of 18-karat gold teeth (he tried 24-karat, but they were too soft), and a set of lead teeth, which were not particularly good for him. These four sets of dentures (the human and animal teeth were mixed) are in the National Museum of Dentistry in Baltimore, Maryland. No other dentures of Washington have been discovered.

MYTH   Queen Marie Antoinette said, "Let them eat cake," when told that the peasants had no bread.

BULLSHIT!   Marie Antoinette never said this line; it was taken from a book by the famous French author Jean-Jacques Rousseau in the years prior to Marie Antoinette becoming queen. This myth arose from hatred against the French royal family in the years following the Revolution.

MYTH   The British King George I of Hanover used English or German when speaking with his cabinet.

BULLSHIT!   I don't know that this is so much a misconception as an assumption that a British monarch would speak English. Those who know history and realize George I was a German prince who spoke no English may then think that "it's obvious" he and his advisors spoke German. The reality is that since his cabinet did not speak German, the lingua franca in the meetings was French.

MYTH   Nero fiddled while Rome burned.

BULLSHIT!   He couldn't have: the fiddle wasn't invented. But that aside, a number of ancient Greek writers tell us that when Nero heard that Rome was alight, he rushed back from his weekend palace to help organize a relief effort. As part of that effort, he opened all of his palaces to provide shelter for the homeless and food for the starving masses. The tragic fires also resulted in new urban development plans to ensure that there would be no repeat.

MYTH   Caligula, the vile and insane ruler of the Roman Empire, is famed for his disgusting habits and his love of his horse Incitatus. His love for Incitatus was so great that we are told he made him a figurative head of the republican government (a consul, to be exact).

BULLSHIT!   Not true at all. Caligula may have been insane, but he wasn't that crazy—such an act would have caused the nation to rise against him. However, he did give the horse a stall of the finest marble, a manger of ivory, and a troop of slaves.

MYTH Edward Murphy said, "Anything that can go wrong, will."

BULLSHIT! What he most likely did say is something along the lines of, "If there's more than one way to do a job, and one of those ways will result in disaster, then somebody will do it that way."

MYTH George Washington was the first head of the locally governed United States.

BULLSHIT! While George Washington was the first president of an independent United States of America, he was actually the 17th head of the locally governing body of the nation. The Continental Congress was a convention of delegates from the 13 colonies who, with the president of the Congress, governed the United States during the American Revolution. The first president of the Continental

Congress was Peyton Randolph, and the most famous was John Hancock, who served twice. The president of the Congress had far less power than the post-independence presidents have, but for all intents and purposes he was the de facto leader of the United States, in rebellion against the king. The last convention of the Continental Congress was on March 2, 1789, two days before the first session of the first United States Congress, and one month before the inauguration of George Washington as the first president of the U.S. government.

MYTH   Lincoln said, "You can fool all of the people some of the time and some of the people all the time, but you can not fool all the people all the time."

BULLSHIT!   There is no record of this in his writings or speeches, and no one really knows where the phrase came from.

MYTH   Lucrezia Borgia was an incestuous murderess.

BULLSHIT!   There is no denying that she was not a saint. However, it is wrong to paint her as a monster. She certainly wielded some power in

MYTH Lady Godiva (the noblewoman, not the chocolate) is said to have ridden naked on horseback through the streets of Coventry to force her husband to lower taxes.

BULLSHIT! Not only did Lady Godiva not do this, it is also unjust to her husband, Leofric, who was a very generous man. Not only did he not overtax his subjects, he contributed vast amounts of his own wealth to charitable causes.

Renaissance Europe, but there is no evidence that she was an incestuous murderess. On the contrary, evidence indicates that she had very strong religious scruples, which would have prevented her from agreeing to such a dalliance, and she is known to have been fond of both her father (the Pope, Alexander VI) and brother until death, strongly opposing the idea that she may have been molested by either of them.

Add to this the fact that she died young at 39, and barely had time to do the many things attributed to her. Victor Hugo is most likely the source of the poison ring story because of his 1833 play in which he depicts her as a "poisonous princess."

MYTH   Christopher Columbus proved the earth is not flat.

BULLSHIT!   We have covered the flat earth myth elsewhere in this book, but in case you missed it, western society has known the earth was a sphere since the ancient Greek times (at least 300 BC), and no one disputed it. The real hindrance to Columbus's plans to explore distant places was a mistaken understanding of the distance to India (Columbus's destination) and not fear of falling off the edge of the earth. Columbus wrongly estimated the distance to be far shorter than what the majority correctly believed, and had he not "discovered" America, he would have run out of supplies. Basically, he had to convince the people with the money that his estimate of the distance was correct when no one else believed him.

MYTH   Cleopatra, Queen of Egypt, was Egyptian.

BULLSHIT!   She was Greek. She was a part
of the Ptolemaic dynasty, which was founded 300
years earlier by Ptolemy I
Soter, the famous general
of Alexander the Great.
Consequently, she primarily
spoke Greek and was the
first Greek ruler of the
Ptolemaic dynasty to make
an attempt to learn Egyptian,

which surely earned her some brownie points with
the locals.

MYTH   There is a curse on the tomb of
Tutankhamun.

BULLSHIT!   There never was a curse of
Tutankhamun. It was made up by a journalist. The
closest thing to it was an inscription on a statue
of Anubis (the god of the dead) in the tomb; the
inscription reads, "It is I who hinder the sand from
choking the secret chamber. I am for the protection of
the deceased."

Lord Carnarvon had been sickly for 20 years prior to entering and leading the excavation of Tutankhamun's tomb, and he eventually died of pneumonia. During the years following the discovery, a handful of the many people involved in the discovery died of quite easily explained causes.

MYTH   Prince Charles will be King Charles III.

BULLSHIT!   It has been officially denied (imagine talking about what name you'll have when your mom dies), but it is believed by many sources based on reports from Prince Charles's friends that he will take George VII as his regal name when he assumes the throne. There are many theories as to why, with the two most popular being that Charles is an unlucky name for English monarchs (Charles I was deposed, and Charles II very nearly so), and that the name George would honor Charles's grandfather George VI.

MYTH   Walt Disney was cryogenically frozen after death so he could be resurrected later in life.

BULLSHIT!   Well, it isn't true at all. Disney is interred at Forest Lawn cemetery in Glendale, California.

MYTH Elizabeth Bathory bathed in the blood of her victims.

BULLSHIT! The famous medieval serial killer, did not bathe in the blood of her victims and the death count (in the hundreds) attributed to her is probably far higher than in reality. Nevertheless she was a sadistic and evil woman.

MYTH Paul Revere rode all the way to Concord on April 16, 1775, to warn American minutemen that the English army was invading.

BULLSHIT! He did not. And Charles Dawes didn't finish the ride either. Dr. Joseph Warren sent Revere and Dawes to Concord to warn John Hancock and Samuel Adams of the invasion, and they and soon met Dr. Samuel Prescott returning home from an evening out. All three were soon captured by the British, but Dawes and Prescott (not Revere) quickly escaped. Some say that Dawes was then thrown from his horse and had to walk back to Lexington, but others claim that after the escape he was lost and had to ride back to Lexington. Of the three, only Prescott made it all the way to Concord.

MYTH   Abraham Lincoln was not a Republican when he won the 1864 presidential election.

BULLSHIT!   By changing the name of his party to "National Union Party," Lincoln was able to court Copperhead (War Democrat) voters, who would never vote Republican. He also selected the only Southern Democrat senator not to resign his seat, Andrew Johnson, to run as his vice president. Despite a convention to raise support for midterm elections, the Republicans in the party joined the ranks of the radicals. By March of 1867, Johnson was the only unionist in office who had not defected, and the National Union Party became a splinter group of the Democratic Party, although ironically the Republicans kept the name of National Union Republicans for a while and consider it part of their lineage.

MYTH   Don Knotts, who played the lovable Barney Fife on *The Andy Griffith Show*, is said to have been a Marine Corps drill instructor during World War II, on Parris Island, South Carolina, of the savage caliber of R. Lee Ermey.

BULLSHIT!　Not true. Knotts enlisted in the Army, not the Marines, and served as a traveling comedian, entertaining troops overseas during World War II, but he never trained anyone and never fired a rifle at anyone.

MYTH　Martin Luther was a great religious reformer and bringer of peace.

BULLSHIT!　In reality he was a bitter anti-Semite. In one of his most famous tracts against the Jews called "On the Jews and Their Lies," he referred to them as a "base, whoring people, that is, no people of God, and their boast of lineage, circumcision, and law must be accounted as

filth." He also suggested that safe conduct for Jews be abolished, that their property be taken from them, and that their houses be burnt to the ground.

MYTH   Vincent van Gogh cut his whole ear off with a razor.

BULLSHIT!   Although most people think that, he actually only removed the tip of it. This is still rather bizarre behavior, but perhaps a little less horrifying than the idea of cutting off the entire ear.

MYTH   Marx said that religion was the opiate of the masses.

BULLSHIT!   What he actually said is, "Religion is the sigh of the oppressed creature, the heart of a heartless world, and the soul of soulless conditions. It is the opium of the people." The bastardized quote makes more sense when it's placed in context with Marx's poetic words.

MYTH   Shakespeare invented about 1,700 words still common in English.

BULLSHIT!   Not true. He anglicized many Latin and Greek words, among other languages, thus coining new English words. But to be invented, a word must have no etymology before a single person imagines it. He is said to have invented "assassination," but what he did was derive it from the medieval Latin *assassinare*, which means "to kill an important person." All of the words he is reputed to have invented can be explained this way. He did, however, devise first-name uses for quite a few words, including Viola, Jessica, and Adrian. The first is Latin, the second Hebrew, the third Greek.

MYTH Richard III had his two nephews killed.

BULLSHIT! Despite what Shakespeare had to say on the matter, there is no evidence for or against the alleged fact.

MYTH Sun Yat-Sen (first provisional president of the Republic of China) is a famous revolutionary who is frequently credited as the man who brought down the last Chinese dynasty.

BULLSHIT! In fact, when the revolution broke out he was in Colorado. As soon as heard about the success of the first revolutionaries he returned to China to cement his place in the history books.

MYTH   Typhoid Mary was the most dangerous woman in America, and she killed hundreds (if not thousands) by infecting them with typhoid.

BULLSHIT!   The story of Typhoid Mary (Mary Mallon) is relatively well-known, and it certainly is true that she carried typhoid fever without catching it herself. It is also true that she caused human deaths as a consequence. What is not true is the enormity of the carnage she left behind her. In fact, Mary, who worked as a cook, caused anywhere from 30 to 53 (different sources cite different numbers) people to catch typhoid, but only three of those people died. When it was first discovered that Mary was the cause of these people becoming ill, she was quarantined.

MYTH   Iron Eyes Cody, the television face of environmental awareness in the 1970s, was a Native American.

BULLSHIT!   He was a first-generation Italian American, born Espera De Corti.

This was for a short time only, as it was felt that it was unfair to quarantine her as others in a similar situation were not quarantined. Mary was allowed to leave on the condition that she stop working as a cook. She accepted the condition but, unable to get a job that paid as well as cooking, she took on a false name and began working at a hospital as a cook. She caused 25 people there to become sick and one died. For this reason, she was arrested and put back in quarantine until she died 18 years later.

MYTH George Washington chopped down his father's cherry tree.

BULLSHIT! That tale was actually made up by Mason Locke Weems, a pastor who wrote *The Life and Memorable Actions of George Washington*. He spiced up Washington's life to make him seem more interesting than he was; in reality, he was a fairly dull and uninspiring man.

MYTH Voltaire said, "I disapprove of what you say, but I will defend to the death your right to say it."

BULLSHIT! What he actually said was, "Think for yourselves and let others enjoy the privilege to do

MYTH Betsy Ross made the first American flag.

BULLSHIT! There is absolutely no evidence of that. It was her grandchildren who made the claim more than 30 years after her death. However, it is true that she was an upholsterer and she did sew some flags for the Navy in 1777.

so too." This is from his "Essay on Tolerance," and it certainly doesn't have quite the same ring to it. The misquote actually comes from a 1907 book called *Friends of Voltaire* by Evelyn Beatrice Hall.

MYTH Karl Marx was Russian.

BULLSHIT! Widely regarded as the father of Communism, Karl Marx was not Russian and, in fact, he never once stepped foot in Russia. He was a German Jew who eventually settled in London, where he remained until his death.

MYTH Einstein failed math at school.

BULLSHIT! It never happened. This is a surprisingly old error that everyone seems to believe. It seems to originate in a 1935 article in the *Ripley's Believe It or Not* magazine, in which the myth first appears in print under the heading "Greatest living mathematician failed in mathematics." Many failing students probably take heart in the myth, thinking that there may be hope for them if Einstein could flunk math and still become a genius, but unfortunately for them, Einstein showed genius from a very young age—including in the field of mathematics. When he was shown the article from the magazine, Einstein laughed and said, "I never failed in mathematics. Before I was 15, I had mastered differential and integral calculus."

MYTH Lawrence of Arabia was a friend of the Arabs.

BULLSHIT! Not so. It goes to show that we should be careful about believing what movies tell us. He wrote in one letter, "I could see that if we won the war, the promises made to the Arabs were dead paper." His apparent friendship with the Arabs was entirely for his own advantage. As an aside, did you know that later in life, Lawrence liked to be whipped regularly for masochistic reasons? And he insisted on being whipped by men only—not women.

MYTH Super celebrity Cher had her lowest set of ribs removed to reduce her waistline.

BULLSHIT! Ever since her career began, the superslim Cher has been accused of having had this done in order to make her skinnier. Not only is this untrue, but it is also untrue of other celebrities such as Elizabeth Taylor and Marilyn Manson, who have also been targets of the same rumor.

MYTH Catherine the Great died while having sex with a horse!

BULLSHIT! It isn't true of course. Catherine was said to have a rather voracious sexual appetite, and when she made enemies it was only natural that they would build a web of lies around that in order to mar her reputation.

MYTH Adolf Hitler was a vegetarian and didn't drink alcohol.

MYTH Einstein was awarded the Nobel Prize for his theory of relativity.

BULLSHIT! Einstein was awarded the Nobel Prize, not for his theory of relativity but for his less well-known work on the photoelectric effect of light.

BULLSHIT! This is a very common myth that seems to be extremely popular—perhaps because it seems ironic that a man who caused one of the worst cases of genocide in history loved animals so much that he wouldn't eat them. But this ironic twist is actually untrue. What is true is that Hitler did prefer a diet of vegetables, but he also had a strong fondness for German sausage and ham, and his cook in the 1930s, Dione Lucas, said that his favorite dish was stuffed baby pigeon. Oh, and to wash it all down, Hitler's drink of choice was beer or watered-down wine. This was also confirmed by Hitler's waiter, Salvatore Paolini.

MYTH   Sir Winston Churchill said that the only traditions observed by the Royal Navy were "rum, sodomy, and the lash."

BULLSHIT!   In fact, when Churchill heard that this statement was being attributed to him, he told his assistant that while he never said the words he wished he had.

MYTH   Gandhi was liberal in all things.

BULLSHIT!   Gandhi, the great liberator, wasn't quite so liberal at home. He refused to allow his sons to get an education, and he even disowned his eldest son because he didn't approve of his marriage. However, as a youth he was definitely very liberal when it came to sex—he had a great deal of it. When he was older, he decided that sex more than three or four times in a marriage was a bad thing and suggested that a law ought to be passed to ban it.

MYTH   Mark Twain is famously quoted as saying, "The only two certainties in life are death and taxes."

BULLSHIT!   This is more a problem of misattribution than of misquotation. Twain did not coin this phrase. Edward Ward, in his 1724 *The Dancing*

Devils wrote, "Death and taxes, they are certain." And Christopher Bullock wrote in his 1716 *The Cobler of Preston* that "'Tis impossible to be sure of anything but death and taxes."

MYTH   George Washington received no compensation for being president.

BULLSHIT!   It is well-known to most people that George Washington refused to be paid as the president of the U.S.—a fact that makes many people look at him with great respect. But in reality he was rather crafty and very greedy. He asked Congress to cover his expenses only—but then he went on a shopping rampage like you wouldn't believe. Instead of taking the $12,000-per-year salary (in 1780 dollars), he charged $449,261.51 in expenses!

MYTH   Napoleon was short.

BULLSHIT!   Contrary to popular belief, much of the reason for the rumors that he was a short man (and thus had to compensate by invading countries and becoming ruler of Europe) comes from the confusion between old French feet and Imperial (British) feet. Measured shortly after his death in 1821, Napoleon was recorded at 5 feet, 2 inches in French feet, which corresponds to 5 feet, 6.5 inches in Imperial feet. This makes Napoleon slightly taller than the average Frenchman of the 19th century. Napoleon's nickname of *le petit caporal* has also perpetuated the rumor, with non-Francophones interpreting *petit* to refer to his height, when it was actually a term of affection referring to his camaraderie with ordinary soldiers.

MYTH   Hitler was an atheist.

BULLSHIT!   One of the most damning criticisms of Hitler and of atheism in general is that Hitler, as an atheist, had no morals and thus could kill freely without care or feeling. Well, Hitler was certainly not an atheist; he was born a Roman Catholic, although how religious he actually was is debatable, and he

MYTH Everyone thinks Machiavelli said "the end justifies the means."

BULLSHIT! But actually he didn't. This is a very liberal interpretation of what Machiavelli actually said: "One must consider the final result." Rather different meanings.

eventually appeared to have abandoned Catholicism for his own form of Germanic paganism. It is clear, though, that Hitler was an evil man, and that his religion was irrelevant to his malevolent personality.

MYTH Darwin states in his book *On the Origin of Species* that humans evolved from apes.

BULLSHIT! Debaters on both sides of the evolution argument are grossly misinformed. He states, quite differently, that apes and humans both evolved from a common ancestor. This seems somewhat less offensive to fundamentalists, and if both sides were to consider it, it might smooth the relationship between fundamentalists and science.

MYTH   Christopher Columbus was Spanish.

BULLSHIT!   He was actually an Italian from Genoa. During his voyages, he didn't discover the United States of America—the closest he got was sightings of Puerto Rico and the U.S. Virgin Islands.

MYTH   John Kennedy was the first to say, "Ask not what your country can do for you, ask what you can do for your country."

BULLSHIT!   American politicians are renowned for plagiarizing their best lines from foreign sources. For example, Abraham Lincoln took the phrase "a government of the people, by the people, and for the people" from the preface of John Wycliff's 1384 edition of the Bible, and Vice President Joe Biden cribbed a few speeches while in the Senate from British Labor Party Member of Parliament Neil Kinnock. This quote, thought by many Americans to be pure Kennedy, was actually from Lebanese writer Khalil Gibran in an article advocating his Lebanese brethren to rebel against the occupying Ottoman Turks.

RELIGION

MYTH   The Catholic Church discourages reading the Bible.

𝔹𝕌𝕃𝕃𝕊ℍ𝕀𝕋!   The Church did not (and does not) do so. The very first Christian Bible was produced by the Catholic Church; it was compiled by Catholic scholars of the 2nd and 3rd centuries and approved for general Christian use by the Catholic Councils of Hippo (393) and Carthage (397). At every mass in the world every day (now and always in the past), the Bible is

read aloud by the priest. In the traditional mass there is one reading from the general body of the Bible, and two from the Gospels. In the modern Catholic mass, there are two readings from the general body of the Bible and one from the Gospels. All Catholic homes have a Bible, and the Bible has always been taught in Catholic schools. This myth has come about because Bibles were often locked away in Churches in the past, but that was not to prevent people having access—it was to prevent them being stolen.

MYTH   Wicca is the world's oldest religion.

BULLSHIT!   As far as scientists can figure out, the world's oldest still-existing religion is Hinduism. Though it is true that the first human faiths were pagan, and Wicca is a re-creation of those religions, Wicca was first popularized by Gerald Gardener in the 1950s. However, it has changed a great deal since then.

MYTH   Jesus was born on the 25th of December.

BULLSHIT!   There is no evidence to that effect. That date was chosen for the celebration of his birth by the Catholic Church, so it would fall nine months after feast day of his conception (the Annunciation), which predated the Christmas season.

MYTH   A typical Muslim is a turbaned dark Arab man with a long beard.

BULLSHIT!   This image depicts the minority of Muslims. Arabs make up only 15 percent of the world's Muslim population. As a matter of fact, the Middle East comes in third as a Muslim region, with east Asia coming in first and Africa coming in at second. Another common misconception is that all Arabs are Muslims. Though the vast majority of Arabs are Muslims (75 percent), there are many other religions that Arabs practice, including Christianity and Judaism.

MYTH   St. Patrick drove all the snakes out of Ireland.

BULLSHIT!   There were never any there to begin with! It is because Ireland is surrounded by water that snakes migrating around the world never reached the emerald isle.

MYTH   Catholics worship Mary and are, therefore, committing idolatry.

BULLSHIT! False. In Catholic theology there are three types of worship: latria, hyperdulia, and dulia. Latria is the highest form of worship (adoration), and it is condemned in the Bible if offered to anyone but God. Dulia and hyperdulia are simple forms of reverence for the saints and Mary. A Catholic who may kneel in front of a statue while praying isn't worshipping the statue or even praying to it, any more than the Protestant who kneels with a Bible in his hands when praying is worshipping the Bible or praying to it. The images of saints (whether they appear in statues or paintings) serve as reminders of the holiness of the person depicted.

MYTH Orthodox Jews have sex through a hole in a sheet.

BULLSHIT! Untrue, and they never have. In fact, according to one rabbi, Shmuley Boteach, "Jewish law does not allow any articles of clothing to be worn during lovemaking," and the use of a sheet would be considered to be a breach of that rule.

MYTH Wiccans like to dress in black, wear a lot of makeup, and show off giant pentacle necklaces.

BULLSHIT! Although some do, most do not. In fact, many Wiccans disregard those who do as "fluffy bunnies," a term used to mean someone who doesn't know what they are doing, or who is in it for the shock value. Pagans and Wiccans can be found in the most ordinary of places: offices, grocery stores, suburbs, you name it. You wouldn't be able to spot them if you tried.

MYTH Adam and Eve eat an apple in the book of Genesis.

BULLSHIT! The fruit is not actually named at all; it is referred to only as the fruit of "the tree of the knowledge of good and evil." The reason this misconception has come about is most likely due to the fact that in Middle English, the word *apple* was used to refer to all fruit and nuts (except berries).

MYTH   Religion is based entirely on faith and not reason.

BULLSHIT!   It is incorrect to say that. In the Middle Ages, St. Thomas Aquinas used rational discourse (based on Aristotle's preceding work) to prove many tenets of Christianity. The result of his labor can be found in the *Summa Theologica*.

Over the centuries, this word has stuck in reference to the Genesis fruit.

MYTH   Catholics aren't Christians.

BULLSHIT!   In fact, Catholics were the first Christians. When reading over the early Christian writings, you can see clearly that their doctrines and teachings are followed in the Catholic Church today. These early writings tell of bishops, virgins living in community (nuns), priests, confession, baptism of infants, the bishop of Rome as head of the Christian religion, and reverence for the saints. Here is a quote from an early Church saint: "[From] Ignatius . . . to the church also which holds the presidency [papacy], in the location of the country of the Romans, worthy of God, worthy of honor, worthy of blessing, worthy of praise, worthy of success, worthy of sanctification, and, because you hold the presidency in love, named after Christ and named after the Father" (St. Ignatius, Letter to the Romans 1:1 [AD 110]).

MYTH   Muslims don't believe in Jesus.

BULLSHIT!   There are many similarities between the historical references of Christianity and Islam. Many people are amazed to find out that, according to Muslim belief, Jesus is one of the greatest messengers of God. One cannot be a Muslim without believing in the virgin birth and the many miracles of Jesus Christ. Jesus is also mentioned in many verses of the Quran and is often used as an example of good virtue and character. However, the main difference between Christianity and Islam is that Muslims do not believe that Jesus was God.

MYTH   The serpent that convinced Eve to take the fruit from the tree of knowledge is referred to as Satan in Genesis.

BULLSHIT!   He is known only as the serpent who was "more subtle than any of the beasts of the earth." Additionally, the term *Lucifer* used in reference to Satan comes from the Vulgate translation of Isaiah 14:12—at no point in the Bible is Satan directly referred to by the name Lucifer.

MYTH   Religion causes conflict and wars.

BULLSHIT!   It is true that some wars have resulted from religion, but in the vast majority of the time prior to last century, there was far more peace and fewer wars. The 20th century was the bloodiest period in human history.

MYTH   In Islamic law, children have no rights.

BULLSHIT!   Contrary to popular belief, children, according to Islamic law, have various rights. One of these is the right to be properly brought up, raised, and educated. Islam encourages children to be brought up well because it is the responsibility of an adult to raise his child to become a moral and ethical adult. Children must also be treated equally. When being given financial gifts they should all receive the same amount, and there should be no preference among them. Children are even permitted to take moderately from their parents' wealth to sustain themselves if the parent declines to give them proper funds for living. In addition, an adult is not allowed to hit a child in the face or hit with anything larger than a pencil.

MYTH   Satan resides in hell.

BULLSHIT!   Amazingly, many Christians believe that Satan is sitting on a throne in hell, laughing at all the agony of the poor damned souls, while his imps and demons run around with pitchforks. None of this is Biblical. Satan is quite frequently described as living on earth, and doing what he does best: corrupting mankind. The tradition of a ruler in hell probably comes from the Greek god Hades, or perhaps from even earlier Egyptian ideas. According to Greek myths, Hades sits on the throne of the Underworld, just as Zeus, his brother, sits on the throne of Olympus.

MYTH   Muslims espouse "kill the infidel" toward all non-Muslims.

BULLSHIT!   This is not a correct portrayal of Islamic law. Islam has always given respect and freedom of religion to all faiths. The Quran says, "God does not forbid you, with regards to those who fight you not for religion nor drive you away out of your

homes, from dealing kindly and justly with them, for god loves those who are just." There are many historical examples of Muslim tolerance toward other faiths. One such example was when the caliph Umar was ruler of Jerusalem from AD 634 to 644. He granted freedom to all religious communities and said that the inhabitants of his city were safe and that their places of worship would never be taken away from them. He also set up courts that were designated to the non-Muslim minorities. Whenever he would visit holy areas, he would ask for the Christian patriarch Sophronius to accompany him.

MYTH   Catholics believe the pope is infallible in all things.

BULLSHIT!   Untrue. Catholics believe that only under certain circumstances is the pope infallible (that is, he can not make a mistake). Catholicism defines three conditions under which the pope is infallible: He must be speaking on morals or faith; it must be binding on the entire church (not just the Roman church, for example); and it must be intended to be a statement invoking the full papal authority, not just personal authority. This means that when the pope is speaking on matters of science, he can make errors.

However, when he is teaching a matter of religion and the other two conditions above are met, Catholics consider that the decree is equal to the Word of God. It cannot contradict any previous declarations and it must be believed by all Catholics.

MYTH   The Catholic Church is opposed to science and rejects evolution.

BULLSHIT!   False. In fact, may great scientific advances have come about through Catholic scholarship and education. The most recent and interesting case is that of Monsignor Georges Lemaître, a Belgian priest who proposed the big bang theory. When Lemaître proposed his theory, Einstein rejected it, causing Monsignor Lemaître to write to him, "Your math is correct, but your physics is abominable." Eventually Einstein came to accept the theory. Furthermore, Catholic schools all around the world (including those in the U.S.) teach scientific evolution as part of their science curriculum.

MYTH   The holocaust was the result of medieval Christianity.

MYTH All religions believe in God or a god.

BULLSHIT! Not true. Buddhism is a good example of this. Buddha was merely a man who developed a system by which a person betters himself through meditation.

BULLSHIT! If that were the case, why was there no Hitler in the Middle Ages? Furthermore, Hitler was most likely an atheist, despite having been born a Catholic.

MYTH Indulgences let you pay to have your sins forgiven.

BULLSHIT! Not true. First of all we need to understand what an indulgence is. The Catholic Church teaches that when a person sins, they get two punishments: eternal (hell) and temporal (punishment on earth while alive, or in purgatory after death). To remove the eternal punishment of hell, a person must confess his or her sins and be forgiven. But the temporal punishment remains. To remove the temporal punishment a person can receive an indulgence. This is a special blessing in which the temporal punishment is removed if a person performs a special act, such as doing good deeds or reading certain prayers. In the Middle Ages, forgers who were working for disobedient bishops would write fake indulgences offering the forgiveness of sins (removal of eternal punishment) in exchange for money, which was often used for church building. Popes had been long trying to end the abuse, but it took at least three centuries for the sale of indulgences to finally end. True indulgences existed from the beginning of Christianity, and the Church continues to grant special indulgences today.

MYTH   Muslims are savages in war.

BULLSHIT!   Quite the contrary is true. When it comes to the conduct of war, there are ten rules that every Muslim army must obey. These rules deal with protecting women, children, and the elderly, avoiding treachery, and generally respecting people. During the Crusades when Saladin defeated the Franks, he honored the defeated Frankish army and supplied them with food and during the Third Crusade when Saladin's enemy, King Richard, fell sick, Saladin sent him a gift of fruits and horses.

MYTH Jihad is about war.

BULLSHIT! The true Arabic meaning of the word *jihad* is "struggle." However, in Islam is the term *jihad* is often used to describe the striving in the way of God. There are many forms of jihad, but the most important ones are *jihad al-nafs* (jihad against ones self), *jihad bil-lisan* (jihad by being vocal), *jihad bil yad* (jihad by using action), and *jihad bis saif* (jihad by using  the sword). Each jihad is ranked differently, and it was reported that Muhammad returned from a battle and said, "We have returned from the lesser jihad (going into battle) to the greater jihad (the struggle of the soul)." This means that a Muslim struggling against himself and his soul is more important than the jihad of going into war. Another misconception is that only when a person dies in war does that person become a martyr. It is actually believed that anyone who is killed in the act of doing anything for the sake of God becomes a martyr. A person who dies while performing pilgrimage in Mecca, a woman who dies while giving birth, and even someone who dies in a car crash while he was on his way to the mosque are all considered martyrs.

MYTH   The three kings are refrred to in the Bible.

BULLSHIT!   No doubt most of us have heard the Christmas carol "We Three Kings of Orient Are," but in fact, the three kings are never referred to as kings in the Bible. Additionally, they are not referred to as a group of three. The only reference to the number three is the number of gifts they carried.

MYTH   Some religions (and even some non-religious people) believe that Emperor Constantine invented the Catholic Church in AD 325.

BULLSHIT!   This is not true. In AD 313, Emperor Constantine announced toleration of Christianity in the Edict of Milan, which removed penalties for professing Christianity. At the age of 40 he converted to Christianity and in 325 he convened the first ecumenical Council of Nicaea. Because of the importance of this council, many people believe that Constantine created the Church, but in fact there had been many councils (though not as large) prior to Nicaea and the structure of the Church already existed. Constantine was at the council merely as an observer, and the bishops and representative of the pope made all of the decisions. Before the Council of Nicaea, priestly celibacy was already the norm, baptism of infants was practiced (as were all seven sacraments), and the structure of priests and bishops was already 300 years old.

MYTH   All Wiccans are witches, and all witches are Wiccans.

BULLSHIT!   All Wiccans are pagans, but not all pagans are Wiccans or witches, and some people are all three. *Pagan* is an umbrella term covering a large group of non-Abrahamic religions, including Wicca, Asatru, Shamanism, Animism, and many others. Wiccans believe in a goddess and a god and reincarnation, but these are specific to Wicca and don't apply to other Pagan religions. Witchcraft is the process of applying willpower through ritual, and can be used in both Paganism and Wicca, but it is not limited to any one religion. Atheists, Christians, Jews, Satanists, and Muslims can all be witches.

MYTH   Catholic Priests can't get married.

BULLSHIT!   In order to clear this one up, we need to first understand the nature of the Catholic Church. Within the universal church, there are sections (also called churches but not in the sense that they are separate)—the most common one is, of course, the Roman (or Latin) Catholic Church. Then there is the Eastern Catholic Church, not to be confused with the Orthodox Church, which is a different religion. Both of these churches fall under the jurisdiction of the pope and believe the same doctrines. There are a lot of differences between the two groups, but these are all in matters of style of worship and certain rules. In the Eastern Church, priests are allowed to be married– but a married priest can't become a bishop. It also happens that occasionally in the Latin Church, pastors who convert from other religions such as the Church of England are allowed to become priests even though they are married, so married priests can be found in all parts of the Roman Catholic Church.

MYTH   The original Buddha was a fat man.

BULLSHIT!   The fat Buddha is a Chinese folk hero from the 10th century who was called Budai,

and is a symbol of contentment. The original Buddha was Siddhartha Gautama, a Nepalese man who was born in the 6th century BC. There have been, through history, 25 men who came to be known as Buddha.

MYTH   Mary Magdalene was a prostitute.

BULLSHIT!

Nowhere in the Bible does it say that Mary Magdalene was a prostitute. In fact, she is barely mentioned at all. Aside from her presence at the resurrection, the only other thing that the Bible mentions is that she was possessed by seven demons.

MYTH   Islamic law dictates harsh treatment of women.

BULLSHIT!   The image of a woman wearing a veil from head to toe, a woman who is treated unfairly, or a woman who is not allowed to drive—these are all too familiar notions when it comes to our perceptions of Islamic women. And while there are Muslim countries that do implement many harsh rulings against women, this should not be portrayed as Islamic law. Many of these countries have cultural differences that go against the teachings of Islam. It should be noted that pre-Islam, Arab women were used for fornication only and had no independence. The birth of a daughter in a family was considered humiliating, and the practice of female infanticide was uncontrolled. When Islam came to being, verses in the Quran condemned the practice of female infanticide. Islam gave back many human rights to women, and Muhammad was even reported as saying that "women are the twin halves of men." A Muslim woman is allowed to reject or accept any suitor for marriage and has the right to seek divorce. There is nothing in Islam that forbids a Muslim woman from exiting her house, and she is allowed to drive. In regards to education, a woman is obliged to seek knowledge, and it is considered a sin if she refuses.

MYTH   The prodigal son refers to someone returning home.

BULLSHIT!   Contrary to popular belief, *prodigal* means "characterized by a profuse or wasteful expenditure"—it is not a reference to leaving or returning.

MYTH The Catholic Church added books to the Bible.

BULLSHIT! This is one of the most widespread misconceptions about the Catholic Church. The Catholic version of the Old Testament differs from the Protestant version in that the Catholic edition contains seven more books than Protestant Bibles. These "extra" books are the reason that many people consider the Church to have added to the Bible, but in fact these books were considered the official canon (list of books) by all Christians until the Protestant Reformation during which Martin Luther (leader of the revolution) removed them. Some of these books contain affirmations of Catholic doctrines which Luther rejected. The reason that the Catholic Church uses the Greek edition is because the apostles used it exclusively in their preaching. Luther decided to use the Jewish Masoretic canon (circa AD 700 to 1000) instead of the Apostolic canon. The seven books he removed were: Tobit, Judith, 1 Maccabees, 2 Maccabees, Wisdom, Ecclesiasticus, and Baruch. Interestingly, Hanukkah is mentioned only in 1 and 2 Maccabees, which are not included in either the modern Jewish or Protestant versions of the Old Testament.

MYTH The Immaculate Conception is a reference to Jesus being born without sin.

BULLSHIT! It is not. Most Christians believe that all people are conceived with original sin (the sin inherited from Adam and Eve) but that Jesus was not. The Catholic Church teaches that Mary was also conceived without sin and this is where the term "Immaculate Conception" came from.

MYTH The papacy is a medieval invention.

BULLSHIT! Not so. The pope is the bishop of Rome, and from the beginning of Christianity he was considered the head of the Church. This fact is alluded to in many of the early Church documents and even in the Bible itself: "And I say to thee: That thou art Peter [Greek for *rock*]; and upon this rock I will build my church" (Matthew 16:18). Peter was the first bishop of Rome, and he led the Church until his death in AD 64, at which point St. Linus became the second pope. St. Irenaeus mentions him here: "The blessed apostles, then, having founded and built up the Church, committed into the hands of Linus the office of the episcopate. Of this Linus, Paul makes mention in the Epistles to Timothy [2 Timothy 4:21]. To him succeeded Anacletus [third pope]; and after him, in the third place from the apostles, Clement [fourth pope] was allotted the bishopric." (Against the Heresies, AD 180.) Pope Benedict XVI is the 265th pope.

MYTH   Wiccans are Satanists and can summon demons.

BULLSHIT!   Elements, yes. Gods and goddesses, yes. Spirits, yes. Demons, absolutely not. Wiccans don't believe in devils, or demons, of any sort. Wicca is an earth-based religion, which means that it values nature and pays respect to the gods and goddesses of the earth and all the creatures that live here. Satan isn't even involved in the Wiccan worldview, which makes worshipping him impossible. Furthermore, most Satanists don't even believe in Satan.

MYTH   Over the centuries, the Bible text has been altered to suit the ideologies of the editors.

BULLSHIT!   While some people believe that, in fact, there have only been a very small number of textual alterations that modern philologists and critics consider intentional changes; most are simply errors in spelling or copying. Bart D. Ehrman, a New Testament textual critic, says, "It would be a mistake . . . to assume that the only changes being made were by copyists with a personal stake in the wording of the text. In fact, most of the changes found in our early Christian manuscripts have nothing to do with theology or ideology. Far and away the most changes are the result of mistakes, pure and simple—slips of the pen, accidental omissions, inadvertent additions, misspelled words, blunders of one sort or another."

MYTH   There was a female pope.

BULLSHIT!   This is one of the more bizarre myths. It goes like this: In the Middle Ages, there was a "Pope Joan," a woman who hid her gender and rose through the ranks of the Church, became a cardinal and was elected pope. No one knew she was a woman until, during a papal procession through the streets of Rome, she went into labor and gave birth to a child. She and the baby were killed on the spot by the mob, enraged at her imposture. This sounds quite strange indeed, and incredibly scandalous if true, but the facts of history show otherwise. The primary proofs that this is all just a fable are: first, the earliest point that we can trace the legend to is the mid-13th century, but the legend didn't really gain wide currency until the late 14th century. No evidence of any kind exists from the 9th century (when Pope Joan was alleged to have reigned), nor do we see any in the 10th through 12th centuries. None of the annals or acts of the popes that were written between the 9th and 13th centuries (and none after that, either) mention her. It's important to remember that even if there had been a female impostor pope, this would just mean that an invalid election had taken place, nothing more.

MYTH There are animal or human sacrifices involved in Wicca.

BULLSHIT! No. It is an earth-based religion, and stresses harming none. That means being nice to all humans, animals, plants, spirits, and yourself. Hurting or killing anything would be against the religion. Wiccans believe that whatever energy you put out, whatever you do to others, will come back to you.

MYTH   Islam was spread by the sword.

BULLSHIT!   Right? Maybe not. Historian De Lacey O'Leary states, "History makes it clear, however, that the legend of fanatical Muslims sweeping through the world and forcing Islam at the point of the sword upon conquered races is one of the most fantastically absurd myths that historians have ever repeated." There is no record in history that shows people being forced by sword point to convert to Islam. When Islam spread through countries, people would set up private churches and synagogues for the non-Muslims they were governing, and because of the good treatment they had received, many non-Muslims would convert. If one considers the small number of Muslims who initially spread Islam to the West, all the way from Spain and Morocco and east from India and China, one would realize that such a small group of people could not force others to be members of a religion against their will. It is also interesting to note that when the Mongols invaded and conquered large portions of the Islamic empire, instead of destroying the religion, they adopted it!

MYTH   There's a special chair the pope must sit on to prove his sex.

BULLSHIT! And just when you thought it couldn't get stranger—how about the myth of the *sedia stercoraria*? The myth: Each pope, when elected, must sit on the sedes stercoraria, a chair with a hole in the center of the seat, without underwear on, in order to have his genitals touched to prove that he is a man. This arose after Pope Joan ruled to make sure that the same mistake would not occur again. The fallacy of the Pope Joan myth is the first step in disproving the myth of the sedes stercoraria. If Joan never existed, the

MYTH Wiccans believe that they have supernatural or superhuman powers.

BULLSHIT! They don't, at least, most don't. *Magick* is the name given to the process of ritually and spiritually aiding in the performance of an action. Anyone can do this. It simply takes the right frame of mind.

need to prove the elected pope male also does not exist. The thrones with holes at St. John Lateran's do indeed exist and were used in the elevation of Pope Pascal II in 1099 (Boureau 1988). In fact, one is still in the Vatican Museums and another is in the Musée du Louvre. They do indeed have holes in the seats. However, as both the seats and their holes predated the Pope Joan story, and indeed Catholicism by centuries, they clearly have nothing to do with a need to check the sex of a pope. It has been speculated that they originally were Roman bidets or imperial birthing stools, which because of their age and imperial links were later used in ceremonies by popes intent on highlighting their own imperial status.

MYTH There are only ten commandments.

BULLSHIT! Considering the importance of the Ten Commandments to so many people, you would think they would have a clear idea of how they are defined, but most people do not. The Bible does not list a consistent set of ten commandments at all. In Exodus, the list includes 14 or 15 statements. Though the Bible does refer to a set of ten rules, it does not mention them in the same sections as the

list commonly known as the Ten Commandments.
Different Christian sects have divided the list of
commandments up differently. The Catholic Church
combines the first three statements into one
commandment, and the Protestants combine the final
two into one statement. To add to the confusion, there
is also another set of ten commandments called the
Ritual Decalogue, which includes laws such as "Do
not cook a kid in its mother's milk."

MYTH All Muslims are terrorists.

BULLSHIT! By far this is the biggest
misconception about Islam. Has anyone else noticed
how when a specific group of people attacks another
group of people it is labeled as a "hate crime," but when

a Muslim opens fire on anybody, it is quickly regarded as "terrorism"? Many political dictators and officials or extremist groups use the name of Islam as a strategy to garner followers and attention when many of their practices go against the true basis of Islam. The media has also portrayed Islam as a cult or a club in which you become a terrorist. However, all over the world people practice Islam in the true form and use it as a way of life. There are many verses in the Quran that go against the idea of terrorism. Some of these verses include, "Fight in the way of Allah those that fight you but do not transgress limits, for God does not love transgressors." This basically means do not fight except in self-defense, and even in doing so do not go beyond defense. Another verse states, "If they seek peace, then you seek peace," which means do not attack people for no reason or kill innocent people. There is nowhere in Islam, whether it be in the Quran or the teachings of Muhammad, that promotes the killing of innocent people.

PHOTO CREDITS

Photo Credits

OTHER ULYSSES PRESS BOOKS

Listverse.com's Ultimate Book of Bizarre Lists: Fascinating Facts and Shocking Trivia on Movies, Music, Crime, Celebrities, History, and More
Jamie Frater, $14.95
From gruesome methods of execution to unusual uses for peanut butter, this book has something for everyone. It offers lists of death-related objects available for purchase online, as well as the weirdest things Michael Jackson owned.

Should I Eat the Yolk?: Separating Facts from Myths to Get You Lean, Fit, and Healthy
Jamie Hale, $14.95
Exercise and nutrition consultant Jamie Hale looks at many diet and exercise advice claims and separates fact from fiction.

The Ultimate Book of Top Ten Lists: A Mind-Boggling Collection of Fun, Fascinating and Bizarre Facts on Movies, Music, Sports, Crime, Celebrities, History, Trivia and More
Compiled from Listverse.com, $15.95
Providing an astonishing array of information, this book contains the best of everything from scientific oddities and historical events to little-known facts about celebrities, films, and books.

What Did We Use Before Toilet Paper?: 200 Curious Questions and Intriguing Answers

Andrew Thompson, $12.95

This witty and compulsive collection of trivia Will captivate and surprise you with its fun and funky revelations like, Why is New York called "the Big Apple"? How do people count cards at casinos? and What keeps the head on a glass of beer?

Married to the Sea: Victorian Newspaper Art Gone Wrong

Drew, $14.95

Reinventing the single-panel cartoon for today's hippest readers, *Married to the Sea* applies modern American culture to stodgy Victorian characters with bizarrely funny results. Reflecting 21st-century attitudes on everything from politics and religion to drinking and sex, the author's shocking captions lay bare the gulf between today and the Victorian era.

To order these books call 800-377-2542 or 510-601-8301, fax 510-601-8307, e-mail ulysses@ulyssespress.com, or write to Ulysses Press, P.O. Box 3440, Berkeley, CA 94703. All retail orders are shipped free of charge. California residents must include sales tax. Allow two to three weeks for delivery.

ABOUT THE AUTHOR

JAMIE FRATER was born and raised in New Zealand. After a stint in the seminary he undertook postgraduate studies at the Royal College of Music in London. Deciding against a career in music he combined his thirst for knowledge and obscure trivia with his passion for computers and launched Listverse. He has been a guest speaker on numerous national radio and television stations in the United States, Canada, and Great Britain and has been featured in numerous national newspapers. He has also compiled two previous tomes of trivia, *The Ultimate Book of Top Ten Lists* and *Listverse.com's Ultimate Book of Bizarre Lists*.